Reparations

Other Books of Related Interest

Opposing Viewpoints Series

Discrimination
Multiracial America
Race in America
Racial Profiling

At Issue Series

Casualties of War
Is Racism a Serious Problem?
Minorities and the Law
Slavery Today

Current Controversies Series

Racial Profiling
Racism
The US Economy

> "Congress shall make no law … abridging the freedom of speech, or of the press."
>
> *First Amendment to the US Constitution*

The basic foundation of our democracy is the First Amendment guarantee of freedom of expression. The Opposing Viewpoints series is dedicated to the concept of this basic freedom and the idea that it is more important to practice it than to enshrine it.

Reparations

Anne Cunningham, Book Editor

Published in 2017 by Greenhaven Publishing

353 3rd Avenue, Suite 255, New York, NY 10010

First Edition

Cover image: Nemeziya/Shutterstock.com

Library of Congress Cataloging-in-Publication Data

Names: Cunningham, Anne, editor.
Title: Reparations / edited by Anne Cunningham.
Description: New York : Greenhaven Publishing, 2017. |
Series: Opposing viewpoints | Includes index.
Identifiers: LCCN ISBN 9781534500310 (pbk.) | ISBN 9781534500259 (library bound)
Subjects: LCSH: African Americans--Reparations--Juvenile literature.
| Slavery--United States--History--Juvenile literature.
Classification: LCC E185.89.R45 C75 2017 | DDC 305.896'073--dc23

Manufactured in the United States of America

Contents

Chapter 3: What Form Should Reparations Take?

Chapter 4: Should Later Generations Be Blamed for Injustices of the Distant Past?

The Importance of Opposing Viewpoints

Perhaps every generation experiences a period in time in which the populace seems especially polarized, starkly divided on the important issues of the day and gravitating toward the far ends of the political spectrum and away from a consensus-facilitating middle ground. The world that today's students are growing up in and that they will soon enter into as active and engaged citizens is deeply fragmented in just this way. Issues relating to terrorism, immigration, women's rights, minority rights, race relations, health care, taxation, wealth and poverty, the environment, policing, military intervention, the proper role of government—in some ways, perennial issues that are freshly and uniquely urgent and vital with each new generation—are currently roiling the world.

If we are to foster a knowledgeable, responsible, active, and engaged citizenry among today's youth, we must provide them with the intellectual, interpretive, and critical-thinking tools and experience necessary to make sense of the world around them and of the all-important debates and arguments that inform it. After all, the outcome of these debates will in large measure determine the future course, prospects, and outcomes of the world and its peoples, particularly its youth. If they are to become successful members of society and productive and informed citizens, students need to learn how to evaluate the strengths and weaknesses of someone else's arguments, how to sift fact from opinion and fallacy, and how to test the relative merits and validity of their own opinions against the known facts and the best possible available information. The landmark series Opposing Viewpoints has been providing students with just such critical-thinking skills and exposure to the debates surrounding society's most urgent contemporary issues for many years, and it continues to serve this essential role with undiminished commitment, care, and rigor.

The key to the series's success in achieving its goal of sharpening students' critical-thinking and analytic skills resides in its title—

Opposing Viewpoints. In every intriguing, compelling, and engaging volume of this series, readers are presented with the widest possible spectrum of distinct viewpoints, expert opinions, and informed argumentation and commentary, supplied by some of today's leading academics, thinkers, analysts, politicians, policy makers, economists, activists, change agents, and advocates. Every opinion and argument anthologized here is presented objectively and accorded respect. There is no editorializing in any introductory text or in the arrangement and order of the pieces. No piece is included as a "straw man," an easy ideological target for cheap point-scoring. As wide and inclusive a range of viewpoints as possible is offered, with no privileging of one particular political ideology or cultural perspective over another. It is left to each individual reader to evaluate the relative merits of each argument—as he or she sees it, and with the use of ever-growing critical-thinking skills—and grapple with his or her own assumptions, beliefs, and perspectives to determine how convincing or successful any given argument is and how the reader's own stance on the issue may be modified or altered in response to it.

This process is facilitated and supported by volume, chapter, and selection introductions that provide readers with the essential context they need to begin engaging with the spotlighted issues, with the debates surrounding them, and with their own perhaps shifting or nascent opinions on them. In addition, guided reading and discussion questions encourage readers to determine the authors' point of view and purpose, interrogate and analyze the various arguments and their rhetoric and structure, evaluate the arguments' strengths and weaknesses, test their claims against available facts and evidence, judge the validity of the reasoning, and bring into clearer, sharper focus the reader's own beliefs and conclusions and how they may differ from or align with those in the collection or those of their classmates.

Research has shown that reading comprehension skills improve dramatically when students are provided with compelling, intriguing, and relevant "discussable" texts. The subject matter of these collections could not be more compelling, intriguing, or urgently relevant to today's students and the world they are poised to inherit. The anthologized articles and the reading and discussion questions that are included with them also provide the basis for stimulating, lively, and passionate classroom debates. Students who are compelled to anticipate objections to their own argument and identify the flaws in those of an opponent read more carefully, think more critically, and steep themselves in relevant context, facts, and information more thoroughly. In short, using discussable text of the kind provided by every single volume in the Opposing Viewpoints series encourages close reading, facilitates reading comprehension, fosters research, strengthens critical thinking, and greatly enlivens and energizes classroom discussion and participation. The entire learning process is deepened, extended, and strengthened.

For all of these reasons, Opposing Viewpoints continues to be exactly the right resource at exactly the right time—when we most need to provide readers with the critical-thinking tools and skills that will not only serve them well in school but also in their careers and their daily lives as decision-making family members, community members, and citizens. This series encourages respectful engagement with and analysis of opposing viewpoints and fosters a resulting increase in the strength and rigor of one's own opinions and stances. As such, it helps make readers "future ready," and that readiness will pay rich dividends for the readers themselves, for the citizenry, for our society, and for the world at large.

Introduction

> *"In the debate about historical injustice, there has been a shift from an individualistic conception...to a collective understanding, which focuses on collective agents, such as nations, as the proper entities that should be held responsible for injustices that occurred in the past."*
>
> *—Sara Amighetti and Alasia Nuti, Ethics and Global Politics, Volume 8, 2015*

In 2016, Georgetown University made the bold decision to attempt to right the wrongs of its past. The university, which had been an active participant in American slavery, announced that it would offer preferential admission to descendants of the 272 enslaved people it sold in 1838 to keep the institution afloat financially. In addition, Georgetown would issue a formal apology for its past actions, change the names of several campus buildings, and create an institute dedicated to the study of slavery. Georgetown was taking responsibility for reprehensible actions that occurred two centuries earlier, undertaken by individuals who are no longer alive, who operated within an institution long since outlawed.

In contemporary American society, the egalitarian ideal that "all men are created equal" as expressed by the framers of the Declaration of Independence is just that–*an ideal.* It exists in uneasy tension with normative conditions that are anything but equal. In fact, our history is rife with violations such as slavery, the genocide of Native Americans, gender inequality, and xenophobia toward immigrants. These many blights indicate that we have never truly been the fair and noble society posited by our optimistic forefathers.

Similarly, the comparatively wealthy nations of Western Europe enjoy high standards of living based on riches accumulated during their various colonial gambits in the so-called third world and global south. This is rarely acknowledged by European powers as a problem. Meanwhile in the rest of the world, we find countless regional aggressors, each eager to conquer and subjugate their neighbors. Of particular concern right now is the Middle East, where violent organizations such as ISIS and Boko Haram threaten human rights in the region and beyond. Their avowed desire to turn the clock back centuries and create a fundamentalist dark age is accompanied by a horrendous trail of kidnapping, rape, and mass murder. However, the fact that flawed Western intervention created the power vacuum into which these rogue states have stepped raises serious concerns as to who is truly culpable for their cancerous rise.

All of these flashpoints of violence, exploitation, and war share one common characteristic: they spread unnecessary misery and death among ordinary, innocent people. Can we as a world community do anything to rectify these past and present horrors? Many argue that yes, indeed we can, and one key place to start is with reparations for victims of these historical injustices.

The views compiled in this volume of Opposing Viewpoints examine the issue of reparations from a multitude of historical, ethical, pragmatic, and material angles. On the historical level, some viewpoints interrogate whether those alive today bear any responsibility for the immoral actions of the long-deceased, a persistent question dogging the reparations discussion, and one to which we will return shortly. On the ethical front, others inquire as to what types of reparations are warranted by the specific transgression in question. Would an acknowledgment by way of formal apology, or a Truth and Reconciliation project, provide sufficient solace to the aggrieved parties? Or is something additional required? Pragmatically speaking, other thinkers debate whether reparations yield unintended negative consequences for all parties and should be avoided for this reason, despite their possible benefit to one subgroup. Finally, even if a valid claim to reparations can be established, the material valuation of such a claim is still contestable on both sides. It's difficult to put a fair price on trans-cultural theft, as evidenced by the Sioux in South Dakota. This group has continually refused offers for compensation for Black Hills land stolen from them long ago.

Above all, the question of whether present generations should shoulder the financial obligation to compensate for the sins of their forefathers haunts the discourse of reparations. This question is perhaps best gracefully sidestepped than answered outright–after all, if the past is always with us, as Faulkner suggests, than the insistence of a level playing field would be an impossible assertion. Moreover, most credible advocates of reparations scoff at the idea of sending checks to random African American or Armenian addresses, to take two examples. Instead, theorists and activists focus on how to address collective and structural inequities, as many of the viewpoints will attest. Going further, we will also encounter a few authors of a more radical theoretical bend. These thinkers eschew brass tacks reparation plans in favor of a total re-think of the concepts of credit and debt.

While the reparations debate provides few easy answers, we hope that these investigations into myriad global cases of victimhood will increase empathy, compassion, and critical thought. It is only through these human qualities that space can be opened for dialogue. Even if true resolution of the past proves impossible, discussion can nonetheless lead us toward eventual progress in the long view.

Chapter 1

Should Countries with Legacies of Civil Rights Injustices Compensate the Descendants of Those They Have Violated?

Chapter Preface

From a skeptical vantage point, human history is nothing more than an unending series of competitive clashes between asymmetrically powerful national, ethnic, religious, and racial groups. These conflicts may be over territory, resources, or belief systems, and sometimes escalate to full-scale war. Given the relatively constant presence of violence, domination, and exploitation, are there instances in which suffering is so egregious as to merit *reparations* for the aggrieved group, either in the form of a symbolic apology, material compensation, or both? If so, who exactly is entitled to reparations? Upon what criteria should they be based, and how should they be administered and distributed? The viewpoints in this chapter examine these questions in the context of nations with histories of human and civil rights abuses. Do countries owe anything to the descendants of those who suffered in the past, and if so, what?

Perhaps the paradigmatic case for reparations is that of African American descendants of former slaves. Those in favor of reparations cite the incalculable wealth produced by slave labor, as well as the ways in which blacks have been systemically excluded from sharing in this wealth, either through overtly segregationist laws or covertly racist public policy. Although slavery was doubtlessly immoral, many have difficulty accepting the idea that providing taxpayer-subsidized reparations to present-day African Americans is a fair way to redress this. After all, we're a nation of immigrants, and many of our families had not yet come to the United States when slavery existed. Objections such as these falsely assume that reparations imply blame and direct responsibility. This is not the case. In fact, most who argue for reparations focus on the longstanding systemic injustice and inequality to which slavery contributed, and from which whites indirectly benefit. Moreover, virtually no one thinks sending checks to individuals is a good idea. Most credible reparation plans focus on collective means of redress, such as scholarship funds, for example.

Other cases for reparations hinge on colonialist exploitation, or one nation's conquest of an ethnic subgroup. Taking the former example, even countries that abolished slavery long ago reaped indirect economic benefit from colonialism—practices that left former colonies with overly cash-crop dependent economies while further enriching already wealthy and powerful nations. Some argue these nations should be liable for the damage they have created and help find and finance solutions.

Although immigration is a separate debate with its own complex contours, this chapter will also examine the intersection of immigration and reparations. Free trade has caused some nations to be impoverished, so it is predictable that many would flee for greener pastures. Thus, some are calling for both open borders and reparations as an ethical imperative. However, this may not be pragmatically viable in our current political climate, rife with rhetoric of building walls. Indeed, as each case for reparations in this chapter illustrates, the gap between ethical clarity and political viability is often quite wide.

Viewpoint 1

"The renewed sense of grievance — which is what the claim for reparations will inevitably create — is neither a constructive nor a helpful message for black leaders to be sending to their communities and to others."

Reparations Have No Rational Basis in Present-Day U.S. Society

David Horowitz

In this viewpoint, right-wing commentator David Horowitz provides ten reasons why reparations are a bad idea for contemporary America. Horowitz believes that African American descendants of former slaves now fully participate in the wealth their ancestors created. In addition, Horowitz cites many of the difficulties in basing a claim to financial compensation solely on race. Arguing that the economic disadvantages suffered by black people are "individual failings," Horowitz seems to deny that systemic racism still exists in America and proffers an exaggerated individualism instead. He asserts that black people have already been repaid in the form of government entitlements and even owe a debt to white Christian abolitionists for ending the institution of slavery–a claim that might appear tone-deaf to some. David Horowitz is the founder of The David Horowitz Freedom Center and author of the book One- Party Classroom.

"Ten Reasons Why Reparations for Blacks Is a Bad Idea for Blacks — and Racist Too," David Horowitz, frontpagemag.com, January 3, 2001. Reprinted by permission.

As you read, consider the following questions:

1. What are some of the key reasons why reparations are unjust for all groups, according to the author?
2. How does the author differentiate those with a "legitimate" claim to reparations from those who do not?
3. What evidence does the author provide to argue that African Americans have in fact already been compensated for slavery?

There Is No Single Group Clearly Responsible For The Crime Of Slavery

Black Africans and Arabs were responsible for enslaving the ancestors of African-Americans. There were 3,000 black slave-owners in the ante-bellum United States. Are reparations to be paid by their descendants too?

There Is No One Group That Benefited Exclusively From Its Fruits

The claim for reparations is premised on the false assumption that only whites have benefited from slavery. If slave labor created wealth for Americans, then obviously it has created wealth for black Americans as well, including the descendants of slaves. The GNP of black America is so large that it makes the African-American community the 10th most prosperous "nation" in the world. American blacks on average enjoy per capita incomes in the range of twenty to fifty times that of blacks living in any of the African nations from which they were kidnapped.

Only A Tiny Minority Of White Americans Ever Owned Slaves, And Others Gave Their Lives To Free Them

Only a tiny minority of Americans ever owned slaves. This is true even for those who lived in the ante-bellum South where only one white in five was a slaveholder. Why should their descendants owe a debt? What about the descendants of the 350,000 Union soldiers who died to free the slaves? They gave their lives. What possible moral principle would ask them to pay (through their descendants) again?

America Today Is A Multi-Ethnic Nation and Most Americans Have No Connection (Direct Or Indirect) To Slavery

The two great waves of American immigration occurred after 1880 and then after 1960. What rationale would require Vietnamese boat people, Russian refuseniks, Iranian refugees, and Armenian victims of the Turkish persecution, Jews, Mexicans Greeks, or Polish, Hungarian, Cambodian and Korean victims of Communism, to pay reparations to American blacks?

The Historical Precedents Used To Justify The Reparations Claim Do Not Apply, And The Claim Itself Is Based On Race Not Injury

The historical precedents generally invoked to justify the reparations claim are payments to Jewish survivors of the Holocaust, Japanese-Americans and African-American victims of racial experiments in Tuskegee, or racial outrages in Rosewood and Oklahoma City. But in each case, the recipients of reparations were the direct victims of the injustice or their immediate families. This would be the only case of reparations to people who were not immediately affected and whose sole qualification to receive reparations would be racial. As has already been pointed out, during the slavery era, many blacks were free men or slave-owners themselves, yet the reparations claimants make no distinction between the roles blacks actually played in the injustice itself. Randall Robinson's book on reparations, *The Debt*, which is the manifesto of the reparations movement is pointedly sub-titled "What America Owes To Blacks." If this is not racism, what is?

The Reparations Argument Is Based On The Unfounded Claim That All African-American Descendants of Slaves Suffer From The Economic Consequences Of Slavery And Discrimination

No evidence-based attempt has been made to prove that living individuals have been adversely affected by a slave system that was ended over 150 years ago. But there is plenty of evidence the hardships that occurred were hardships that individuals could and did overcome. The black middle-class in America is a prosperous community that is now larger in absolute terms than the black underclass. Does its existence not suggest that economic adversity is the result of failures of individual character rather than the lingering after-effects of racial discrimination and a slave system that ceased to exist well over a century ago? West Indian blacks in America are also descended from slaves but their average incomes are equivalent to the average incomes of whites (and nearly 25% higher than the average incomes of American born blacks). How is it that slavery adversely affected one large group of descendants but not the other? How can government be expected to decide an issue that is so subjective—and yet so critical—to the case?

The Reparations Claim Is One More Attempt To Turn African-Americans Into Victims. It Sends A Damaging Message To The African-American Community.

The renewed sense of grievance—which is what the claim for reparations will inevitably create—is neither a constructive nor a helpful message for black leaders to be sending to their communities and to others. To focus the social passions of African-Americans on what some Americans may have done to their ancestors fifty or a hundred and fifty years ago is to burden them with a crippling sense of victim-hood. How are the millions of refugees from tyranny and genocide who are now living in America going to receive these claims, moreover, except as demands for special treatment, an extravagant new handout that is only necessary because some blacks can't seem to locate the ladder of opportunity within reach of others—many less privileged than themselves?

Reparations To African Americans Have Already Been Paid

Since the passage of the Civil Rights Acts and the advent of the Great Society in 1965, trillions of dollars in transfer payments have been made to African-Americans in the form of welfare benefits and racial preferences (in contracts, job placements and educational admissions)—all under the rationale of redressing historic racial grievances. It is said that reparations are necessary to achieve a healing between African-Americans and other Americans. If trillion dollar restitutions and a wholesale rewriting of American law (in order to accommodate racial preferences) for African-Americans is not enough to achieve a "healing," what will?

What About The Debt Blacks Owe To America?

Slavery existed for thousands of years before the Atlantic slave trade was born, and in all societies. But in the thousand years of its existence, there never was an anti-slavery movement until white Christians—Englishmen and Americans—created one. If not for the anti-slavery attitudes and military power of white Englishmen and Americans, the slave trade would not have been brought to an end. If not for the sacrifices of white soldiers and a white American president who gave his life to sign the Emancipation Proclamation, blacks in America would still be slaves. If not for the dedication of Americans of all ethnicities and colors to a society based on the principle that all men are created equal, blacks in America would not enjoy the highest standard of living of blacks anywhere in the world, and indeed one of the highest standards of living of any people in the world. They would not enjoy the greatest freedoms and the most thoroughly protected individual rights anywhere. Where is the gratitude of black America and its leaders for those gifts?

The Reparations Claim Is A Separatist Idea That Sets African-Americans Against The Nation That Gave Them Freedom

Blacks were here before the *Mayflower*. Who is more American than the descendants of African slaves? For the African-American community to isolate itself even further from America is to embark on a course whose implications are troubling. Yet the African-American community has had a long-running flirtation with separatists, nationalists and the political left, who want African-Americans to be no part of America's social contract. African Americans should reject this temptation.

For all America's faults, African-Americans have an enormous stake in their country and its heritage. It is this heritage that is really under attack by the reparations movement. The reparations claim is one more assault on America, conducted by racial separatists and the political left. It is an attack not only on white Americans, but on all Americans—especially African-Americans.

America's African-American citizens are the richest and most privileged black people alive—a bounty that is a direct result of the heritage that is under assault. The American idea needs the support of its African-American citizens. But African-Americans also need the support of the American idea. For it is this idea that led to the principles and institutions that have set African-Americans—and all of us—free.

> *"The reparations claim therefore is not a matter for individuals, and no one is suggesting that cheques be sent to living people. Rather, the claim focuses on the different development trajectories between the colonies and the imperial powers."*

Former Colonialist Powers Owe Assistance to Their Former Colonies

Tim Lockley

In this viewpoint, Tim Lockley contends that the underdevelopment Caribbean nations now face is a direct result of colonialist history and an economic system that benefited Europe at the expense of the formerly colonized. Although Lockley stops short of recommending direct reparation payments to individuals, he reasons the data merits some ameliorative action. To this end, several Caribbean nations have formed a commission on reparations. However, the issue remains a non-starter for British leadership. This is unlikely to change, as pinning accountability on living descendants of slaveholding ancestors is a difficult task. In addition, the false perception that other nations need aid more than the Caribbean stand in the way of those seeking a form of reparations. Tim Lockley is a historian specializing in race relations and slavery, and teaches at the University of Warwick.

"Britain rules out slavery reparations—but should the Caribbean get more aid?," Tim Lockley, The Conversation, October 1, 2015. http://theconversation.com/britain-rules-out-slavery-reparations-but-should-the-caribbean-get-more-aid-48450.

As you read, consider the following questions:

1. What are some important points the author makes in the case for reparations in the Caribbean context?
2. Has there been precedent for reparations payouts in the past?
3. In lieu of reparations, how might the relatively low GDP per capita of Caribbean nations be addressed?

Caribbean countries are keeping the case for slavery reparations at the forefront of the international political agenda, and have established a commission on the issue. But after protesters raised the matter during David Cameron's recent visit to Jamaica, the British prime minister ruled out the payment of reparations for his country's role in the international slave trade in a speech to the Jamaica's parliament.

On the one hand Caribbean nations point to the crime of the African slave trade and the plantation systems that were instituted in the colonies. Millions of Africans were forcibly transported to the Americas over the course of about 300 years. Once there they were beaten, tortured, raped and sometimes murdered in the pursuit of profit. European nations were the principal beneficiaries of the system.

On the other hand, Europeans nations claim that they cannot be held liable for what their ancestors did hundreds of years ago, in an age when different morals held sway.

Reparations for previous national crimes are not unprecedented. Germany paid out significant sums following World War II, and more recently Britain paid compensation to Kenyans tortured during the Mau-Mau uprising in the 1950s. Crucially, however, these offences were comparatively recent and the claims made by those who had directly suffered.

Shattered Trajectories

The reparations for slavery debate is different. The British abolished slavery in the 1830s, emancipating those who had been enslaved. Other countries did the same during the 19th century, ending with Brazil in 1888. There are no living former slaves in the Americas. Equally, those who owned slaves are long dead.

The reparations claim therefore is not a matter for individuals, and no one is suggesting that cheques be sent to living people. Rather the claim focuses on the different development trajectories between the colonies and the imperial powers.

The wealth of the colonies, produced by slaves, flowed into the European nations, helping to drive the industrial revolution. Colonies, by contrast, suffered under-investment in education and infrastructure and had poorly diversified economies. When political independence came in the 1950s and 1960s, the new nations were overly reliant on cash crop agriculture and had barely literate populations.

It's easy for critics to argue that in the half century since many Caribbean nations gained independence they should have sorted themselves out. Surely 50 years is enough time to develop into a modern nation state? Aren't the calls of politicians for reparations simply to cover up their own failings to deliver a better standard of living for their own people? Blaming an external enemy has long been the refuge of those needing to shore up domestic support.

Yet the legacy of colonialism can be clearly seen in data for GDP per capita from the International Monetary Fund. The UK has GDP per capita that is three times that of Barbados and ten times that of Jamaica. The Caribbean nations are often indebted, struggling to finance the health and educational infrastructure of a modern state. Much of the work of the Caricom Reparations Commission focuses on these developmental issues, arguing that Britain and the other nations have a moral obligation to support the long-term development of their former colonies that were hampered by the outset by the legacies of slavery.

Caribbean Misses Out

The UK's overseas aid budget is more than £11 billion annually, yet very little actually goes to the Caribbean in bilateral aid. In 2013, 54.1% of UK bilateral aid went to Africa, 42.1% to Asia and 3.2% to the Americas. Education and health programmes in South Asia and Africa tend to rank far above the West Indies in attracting the support of politicians.

Part of the problem lies in perception. The Caribbean does not seem like a poor part of the world to tourists who visit its resorts and palm-fringed beaches. To them it seems far more like a luxurious paradise. Yet, one does not have to travel far beyond the hotel gates to find exactly the same sort of poverty so visible in Africa or Asia. Perhaps Cameron's visit to Jamaica will bring home to him the fact that the development needs of Britain's former West Indian colonies are also very significant.

Cameron has not embraced the reparations movement with open arms, particularly at a time when he's under political pressure at home from UKIP, which already wants to slash the foreign aid budget. If he acknowledges the case for reparations from the Caribbean, then surely more claims would come from the Asian sub-continent and Africa which were equally exploited in the colonial era.

But perhaps a subtle shift will develop in the future, whereby the current overseas aid budget is broadened to include more for the Caribbean. In some senses, the argument has already been won—Britain tends to direct most of its bilateral aid to former colonies, focusing on health and education just like the reparations commission wishes—it's just that the Caribbean has tended to miss out.

The government might also encourage UK businesses and NGOs to do more to support the postgraduate studies of the next generation of West Indian doctors, engineers, lawyers, teachers and politicians. The Reparations Commission is unlikely to get the public victory is wants, but it might achieve many of its aims via quieter policy shifts that could have a significant impact.

Russian Lawmakers Take Aim At Germany

MOSCOW — A Russian lawmaker is calling for Germany to pay trillions of euros in reparations for World War II.

Mikhail Degtyaryov, a State Duma deputy with the nationalist Liberal Democratic Party, told the pro-Kremlin daily Izvestia that he has called for a working group to determine how much Berlin should pay Moscow. He said the figure should be "no less than 3 trillion-4 trillion euros."

Degtyaryov's move comes less than a week after State Duma speaker Sergei Naryshkin asked a parliamentary committee to consider a resolution condemning what he called West Germany's "annexation" of East Germany when the two states unified in 1990.

The recent vitriol against Germany, not long ago Russia's closest ally in Europe, reflects a dramatic deterioration in relations between Berlin and Moscow due to the Ukraine crisis.

Moscow-based political analyst Dmitry Oreshkin said such "mad statements" were largely for domestic consumption but were also symptomatic of Russia's dismal relations with Europe.

"These kinds of rhetorical exercises are aimed at worsening relations with Europe and the restoration of the Iron Curtain, at least in psychological terms," Oreshkin, who is often critical of the Kremlin and sympathetic to the opposition, said.

Speaking to Izvestia, Degtyaryov said that the Soviet Union forgave East Germany's reparation debt but added that no such agreement had been struck after Germany's reunification in 1990.

"Effectively, Germany hasn't paid the USSR any reparations for the destruction and brutality during the Great Patriotic War," he said, using the common Russian name for World War II.

In fact, Germany paid reparations to the United Kingdom, France, and the Soviet Union in the form of forced labor, dismantled industrial installations, and raw materials as agreed by the Allied forces at the Yalta and Potsdam conferences in 1945.

Postwar Germany was carved up into Allied occupation zones and Moscow was allowed to strip material reparations—consisting of heavy industry, goods, and land—from the country's Soviet-controlled East. Moscow additionally received 10 percent of industrial equipment from the western zones.

The Soviet Union also used hundreds of thousands of German civilians and millions of prisoners of war as forced labor.

In 1953, Moscow terminated material reparations from East Germany, which by then was a Soviet satellite.

"Germany is unlikely to pay anything," Russian historian Sergei Fokin told Izvestia. "But we need to remember this history."

Viewpoint 

> *"Reparations also represent a concrete, material, permanent, and thus not merely rhetorical recognition by perpetrator groups or their progeny of the ethical wrongness of what was done, and of the human dignity and legitimacy of the victim groups."*

Victimized States Need Compensation from Those Who Have Reaped the Benefit

Henry Theriault

In the following viewpoint, Henry Theriault traces the abuses and exploitation long suffered by weaker nations at the hands of comparatively more powerful ones—usually, though not always, of European origin. Theriault argues that the marginalization and diminished status persisting in some nations is a direct result of immoral and illegal actions suffered in the past. According to the doctrine of "necessary fairness," victimized nations deserve the meaningful apology material compensation would represent. For example, since the Turkish state has benefitted from crimes against Armenia, it is obligated to redress these wrongs, despite the fact that present-day Turkish citizens are not directly responsible. Theriault links this particular case to a global movement advocating for reparations on human rights grounds. Henry C. Theriault earned his Ph.D. in philosophy in 1999 from the University of Massachusetts,

"The Global Reparations Movement and Meaningful Resolution of the Armenian Genocide" by Henry Theriault, published in the *Armenian Weekly* April 2010 Magazine. Reprinted by permission.

with a specialization in social and political philosophy. He is currently a professor in and chair of the Philosophy Department at Worcester State College, where he has taught since 1998.

As you read, consider the following questions:

1. What common experiences and challenges do the various victimized groups identified by the author share?
2. What are some of the reasons why a century old Turkish Armenian conflict merits reparations in the present, according to the author?
3. What are the specifics of the Armenian Genocide Reparations Study Group's (AGRSG) recommendations for financial and territorial reparations?

Over the past half millennium, genocide, slavery, Apartheid, mass rape, imperial conquest and occupation, aggressive war targeting non-combatants, population expulsions, and other mass human rights violations have proliferated. Individual processes have ranged from months to centuries. While the bulk of perpetrator societies have been traditional European countries or European settler states in Australia, Africa, and the Americas, Asian and African states and societies are also represented among them. These processes have been the decisive force shaping the demographics, economics, political structures and forces, and cultural features of the world we live in today, and the conflicts and challenges we face in it. For instance, understanding why the population of the United States is as it is—why there are African Americans in it, where millions of Native Americans have "disappeared" to, why Vietnamese and Cambodian people have immigrated to the United States, etc.—requires recognizing the fundamental role of genocide, slavery, and aggressive war in shaping the United States and those areas, such as sub-Saharan Africa and Southeast Asia, affected by it.

Around the globe, those in poverty, those victimized by war after war, small residuals of once numerous groups, and others have recognized that their current difficulties, their current misery, is a direct result of these powerful forces of exploitation, subjugation, and destruction. Out of the compelling logic of "necessary fairness"—fair treatment that is necessary to their basic material survival and to their dignity as human beings—many have recognized that the devastating effects of these past wrongs must be addressed in a meaningful way if their groups and societies can hope to exist in sustainable forms in the future. This recognition has led to various reparations movements. Native Americans lay claim to lands taken through brutal conquest, genocide, and fraud. African Americans demand compensation for their contribution of a significant share of the labor that built the United States, labor stolen from them and repaid only with cruelty, violence, and individual and community destruction. Formerly colonized societies whose people's labor was exploited to build Europe and North America, whose raw materials were stolen to provide the materials, and whose societies were "de-developed," now struggle to survive as the global Northern societies built on their losses capitalize on the previous thefts to consolidate their dominance. And so on.

In the past decade those engaged in these various struggles have begun to recognize their common cause and a global reparations movement has emerged. In 2005, for instance, Massachusetts' Worcester State College held an international conference on reparations featuring renowned human rights activist Dennis Brutus, with papers on reparations for South African Apartheid; African American slavery, Jim Crow, and beyond; Native American genocide and land theft; the "comfort women" system of sexual slavery implemented by Japan; the use of global debt as a "post-colonial" tool of domination; and the Armenian Genocide. While there are dozens if not hundreds of major reparations processes in the world today, it will be instructive to consider these cases in detail, as illustrations of these many struggles.

U.S. slavery destroyed African societies and exploited and abused violently millions of human beings for 250 years. At its dissolution, it pushed former slaves into the U.S. economy without land, capital, and education. Initial recognition of the need to provide some compensation for slavery in order to give former slaves a chance toward basic economic self-sufficiency gave way to violent and discriminatory racism. Former slaves were forced into the economic order at the lowest level. Wealth is preserved across generations through inheritance. Those whose people begin with little and who do not enslave or exploit others will remain with little. Reparations for African Americans recognizes that the poverty, discrimination, and other challenges facing African Americans today result from injustices more than 100 years ago that have never been corrected, and the subsequent racist violence and discrimination that has preserved the post-slavery status quo every since.

The South African case revolved around the fact that, as the world had divested from South Africa in the 1980's, the Afrikaner government borrowed money, especially from Switzerland, to continue to finance Apartheid. Against the international embargo, bankers' loans paid for the guns and other military hardware that were used to kill black activists and keep their people in slavery. The fall of Apartheid did not mean an end to the debt. Today's South Africans live in poverty as their country is forced to pay off the tens of billions of U.S. dollars in loans incurred to keep them in slavery before. They pay yet further billions for the pensions of Afrikaner government, military, and police officials living out their days in quiet comfort after murdering, torturing, and raping with impunity for decades. What is more, U.S. and other corporations drew immense profits from South African labor. Many victims of Apartheid reject the loan debt and demand reparation for all they suffered and all that was expropriated from them as the just means for bringing their society out of poverty. After years of refusal, the South African government itself has recently reversed its position based on the desire to curry favor with large corporations and has begun to support U.S. court cases for reparations from corporations enriched by Apartheid.

In the aftermath of decolonization, societies devastated by decades or centuries of occupation, exploitation, cultural and familial destruction, and genocide were left in poverty and without the most basic resources needed to meet the minimum needs of their people. Forced suddenly to compete with those who had enriched themselves and grown militarily and culturally powerful through colonialism, they had no chance. Their only option was to borrow money in the hope of "catching up." But corrupt and selfish leaders diverted billions to private bank accounts (with winks from former colonial powers), invested in foolish and irrelevant public works projects, and otherwise misappropriated money that was supposed to help these societies. Loan makers, such as the International Monetary Fund and World Bank, imposed conditions to push these societies into a new servitude to the economies of the United States and other great powers. Servicing the loans that have not helped their economies develop now means sacrificing basic human services and healthcare in these desperate societies and accepting extensive outside control of their societies to benefit former colonizers and multinational corporations at the expense of further degradation of the dignity and material conditions of their populations. The Jubilee movement calls for debt cancellation as a crucial step toward justice for the devastation of colonialism and post-colonialism and a path toward a sustainable and fair global economy.

Former comfort women have long faced assaults on their dignity in their home countries and by Japan. They were often impoverished by their devastating experiences of being raped on average thousands of times in permanent rape camps as sexual slaves to the Japanese military. Physical damage from incessant forced intercourse and the brutal violence soldiers subjected them to, the aftermath of coerced drug addiction, and intense psychological trauma have frequently followed the women into their old age. They have needed medical care as well as acknowledgment of the inhuman injustice done to them. In the early 1990's, surviving "comfort women" began calling for reparations to address the effects of what they had suffered.

Native Americans and Armenians share certain similarities in their past experiences and challenges today, from being crushed by competing as well as sequential imperial power-games and conquests, and a series of broken or unfair treaties, to a history of being subject to massacre, sexual violence, and societal destruction. Members of both groups have been sent on their "long marches" to death. In the aftermath of active genocide through direct killing and deadly deportation, even the remnants of these peoples on their own lands have been erased, through the raiding and destruction of hundreds of thousands to millions of Native American graves as a policy of the U.S. "scientific" establishment, and the continuing destruction of remaining Armenian Church and other structures throughout Turkey. For Native Americans, the continuing expropriation of land and resources, the blocking of Native American social structures and economic activity, and the dramatic demographic destruction (an estimated 97 percent in the continental United States) has left behind a set of Indian nations subject to the whims of the U.S. government and struggling to retain identity and material survival in a hostile world. Reparations, particularly of traditional lands, are essential to the survival of Native peoples and cultures. Similarly, from its status as the major minority in the Ottoman Empire a century ago, today an Armenian population of below 3 million in the new republic faces a Turkey of 70 million with tremendous economic resources built on the plunder of Armenian wealth and land—through genocide and the century of oppression and massacre that preceded it—and tremendous military power awarded it through aid from the United States in recognition of its regional power—also gained through genocide. The Armenian Diaspora of perhaps five million is dispersed across the globe and slowly losing cohesion and relevance as powerful forces of assimilation and fragmentation take their toll. Reparations in the form of compensation for the wealth taken, which in many cases can be traced to Turkish families and business today, and lands depopulated of Armenians and thus "Turkified" through genocide, are crucial to the viability of Armenian society and culture in the future. Without the kind of secure cradle the Treaty of Sevres was supposed to give Armenians, true regeneration is impossible: Turkish power, still violently hostile to Armenians, grows each day, as the post-genocide residual Armenia degenerates.

Of course, reparations are not simply about mitigating the damage done to human collectivities in order to make possible at least some level of regeneration or future survival, however important this is. Reparations also represent a concrete, material, permanent, and thus not merely rhetorical recognition by perpetrator groups or their progeny of the ethical wrongness of what was done, and of the human dignity and legitimacy of the victim groups. They are the form that true apologies take, and the act through which members who supported the original assault on human rights or who benefited from it—economically, politically, militarily, culturally, and in terms of the security of personal and group identity—decisively break with the past and refuse to countenance genocide, slavery, Apartheid, mass rape, imperial conquest and occupation, aggressive war focused on civilians, forced expulsions, or any other form of mass human rights violation.

It is with both dimensions in mind that in 2007 Jermaine McCalpin, a political scientist with a recent Ph.D. from Brown University specializing in long-term justice and democratic transformation of societies after mass human rights violations; Ara Papian, former Armenian ambassador to Canada and expert on the relevant treaty history and law; Alfred de Zayas, former senior lawyer with the Office of the UN High Commissioner for Human Rights and Chief of Petitions, and currently professor of international law at the Geneva School of Diplomacy and International Relations; and I came together to study the issue of reparations for the Armenian Genocide in concrete terms. The Armenian Genocide Reparations Study Group's (AGRSG) work has culminated in a draft report on the legal, treaty, and ethical justifications for reparations and offers concrete proposals for the political process that will support meaningful reparations. The following are some of the elements of the AGRSG findings, arguments, and proposals.

International law makes clear that victim groups have the right to remedies for harms done to them. This applies to the Armenian Genocide for two reasons. First, the acts against Armenians were illegal under international law at the time of the genocide. Second, the 1948 UN Convention on the Prevention and Punishment of Genocide applies retroactively. While the term "genocide" had not yet been coined when the 1915 Armenian Genocide was committed, the Convention subsumes relevant preexisting international laws and agreements, such as the 1899 and 1907 Hague Conventions. Since the genocide was illegal under those conventions, it remains illegal under the 1948 Convention. What is more, the current Turkish Republic, as successor state to the Ottoman Empire and as beneficiary of the wealth and land expropriations made through the 1915 genocide, is responsible for reparations.

While the 1920 Sevres Treaty, which recognized an Armenian state much larger than what exists today, was never ratified, some of its elements retain the force of law and the treaty itself is not superseded by the 1923 Treaty of Lausanne. In particular, the fixing of the proper borders of an Armenian state was undertaken pursuant to the treaty and determined by a binding arbital award. Regardless of whether the treaty was ultimately ratified, the committee process determining the arbital award was agreed to by the parties to the treaty and, according to international law, the resulting determination has legal force regardless of the ultimate fate of the treaty. This means that, under international law, the so-called "Wilsonian boundaries" are the proper boundaries of the Armenian state that should exist in Asia Minor today.

Various ethical arguments have been raised against reparations generally and especially for harms done decades or centuries in the past. Two of particular salience are that (1) a contemporary

Slave Descendants Are Not Victims

Imagine that, years in the future, thousands of special "slavery reparations courts" are set up throughout America, charged with the task of trying to sort out who gets compensation for the wrongs of slavery, and who pays. People are demanding government money based on some claim to African American ancestry, even light-skinned people with a trace of African American blood. Others are there to challenge having to pay for the reparations, such as recent immigrants, Latinos, Asian Americans and Caucasian Americans whose ancestors arrived in America long after slavery ended.

Sound far-fetched? It is not. The issue of slave reparations has gone from being on the fringes of American politics to the front and center today. Political momentum for it is strong within the black community, and many whites embrace the issue as well. A growing number of local, state and national politicians support creating a massive government program that would pay billions of taxpayer dollars to slave descendants. In addition, the reparations coalition is orchestrating aggressive media and litigation campaigns to force corporations that allegedly profited from slavery to make huge payouts.

One has to ask why this is happening now, more than 140 years after slavery ended. A critical dynamic fueling the slave reparations movement is a phenomenon common to advocacy groups: once they reach their goal, their original reason for being is no more, but they do not want to disband so they seek another issue. This is the dilemma confronting the civil rights movement. In the 1960s, civil rights activists achieved the worthy goal of ending state-sponsored discrimination. Then they moved on to more dubious things such as racial quotas. Having succeeded, they are now embracing the cause of slave reparations.

It goes hand-in-hand with the current political and legal climate in America. People increasingly see themselves as victims of some alleged wrong, and politicians and juries are taking their side. In the wake of the litigation explosion in America, moreover, trial lawyers keep pushing the envelope as to how much they can get away with, and they are succeeding.

> However surreal or absurd the issue of slave reparations sounds, it is vital that Americans start taking the issue seriously. Though the issue of slave reparations seems frivolous, the political movement coalescing behind it is not.
>
> **Introduction from "The Case Against Slave Reparations," Peter Flaherty and John Carlisle, National Legal and Policy Center, October 2004.**

state and society that did not perpetrate a past mass human rights violation but merely succeeded the state and society that did, does not bear responsibility for the crime nor for repairing the damage done, for this would be penalizing innocent people; and (2) those pursuing Armenian Genocide land reparations are enacting a territorial nationalist irredentism that is similar to the Turkish nationalism that drove Turkification of the land through the genocide, and is thus not legitimate.

To the first objection, the report responds that because current members of Turkish society benefit directly from the destruction of Armenians in terms of increased political and cultural power as well as a significantly larger "Turkish" territory and a great deal of personal and state wealth that has been the basis of generations of economic growth, they have a link to the genocide. While they cannot be blamed morally for it, they are responsible for the return of wealth and making compensation to Armenians for other dimensions of the genocide. To the second objection, the report responds that the lands in question became "Turkish" precisely through the ultranationalist project of the genocide. Retaining lands "Turkified" in this way indicates implicit approval of that genocidal ultra-nationalism, while removing Turkish control is the only route to a rejection of that ideology.

In addition to the legal, political, and ethical arguments justifying reparations, the report also proposes a complex model for the political process for determining and giving reparations. The report makes clear that material reparations and symbolic reparations, including an apology and dissemination of the truth about what happened in 1915, as well as rehabilitation of the perpetrator society are crucial components of a reparations process if it is to result in a stable and human rights-respecting resolution. The report proposes convening an Armenian Genocide Truth and Reparations Commission with Turkish, Armenian, and other involvement that will work toward both developing a workable reparations package and a rehabilitative process that will tie reparations to a positive democratic, other-respecting transformation of the Turkish state and society. As much as reparations will be a resolution of the Armenian Genocide legacy, they will also be an occasion for productive social transformation in Turkey that will benefit Turks.

Finally, the report makes preliminary recommendations for specific financial compensation and land reparations. The former is based in part on the detailed reparations estimate made as part of the Paris Peace Conference, supplemented by additional calculations for elements not sufficiently covered by the conference's estimation of the material financial losses suffered by Armenians. The report also discusses multiple options regarding land return, from a symbolic return of church and other cultural properties in Turkey to full return of the lands designated by the Wilsonian arbitral award. The report includes the highly innovative option of allowing Turkey to retain political sovereignty over the lands in question but demilitarizing them and allowing Armenians to join present inhabitants with full political protection and business and residency rights. This model is interesting in part because it suggests a human rights-respecting, post-national concept of politics that some might see as part of a transition away from the kinds of aggressive territorial nationalisms—such as that which was embraced by the Young Turks—that so frequently produce genocide and conflict.

On May 15, 2010, the AGRSG will present its draft report formally in a public event at George Mason University's Institute for Conflict Analysis and Resolution in Arlington, Va.

VIEWPOINT 4

> *"Providing reparations for immigrants entering under open borders could eventually help instill the idea in Americans' hearts and minds that restrictions have constituted a great sin against a large portion of humanity."*

Immigrants Deserve Reparations and Open Borders

Joel Newman

The case for reparations has been taken up successfully by formerly interned Japanese Americans. Moreover, movements to compensate African Americans and Native Americans are gaining traction as well. Using these successes as his point of departure, Joel Newman argues the viewpoint that immigrants also deserve reparations. The United States has a long history of systemically oppressing specific ethnic groups and restricting access to potential immigrants. To redress these wrongs, Newman suggests that the United States should not only open its borders but also provide immigrants with access to government services and a cash allowance. Although he claims this plan is both morally necessary and for the greater good, the author also acknowledges the difficulties inherent in this plan, including a lack of consensus among left-leaning immigration advocates regarding such reparations. Joel Newman teaches in Beaverton, Oregon.

"Open Borders Plus Reparations," Joel Newman, Open Borders: The Case, January 31, 2016. http://openborders.info/blog/open-borders-reparations/.

As you read, consider the following questions:

1. What are the author's main arguments for opening borders and lifting restrictions on immigration?
2. Why is the U.S. government responsible for providing reparations to immigrants, according to the article?
3. How does the article suggest reparations for immigrants should be distributed?

Open borders is a tough sell in Western countries. Generations of closed borders and anti-open borders propaganda has led most Westerners to conclude that having open borders is reckless and potentially disastrous for receiving countries. My fellow bloggers and I have worked hard to reverse this current of thought, but much work still needs to be done to help realize our goal. So why burden ourselves by also pushing for reparations for immigrants on top of open borders, as I advocate in this post? Because it is morally warranted. (See here for my post that outlines why open borders itself is warranted: http://openborders.info/blog/favorite-arguments-open-borders. In this post the focus is on open borders plus reparations in the U.S. context, but the same arguments apply universally.)

In the United States, reparations for harm committed against certain ethnic groups by the government have periodically been considered. Decades after the government interned over one hundred thousand Japanese-Americans during War II, the U.S. provided monetary reparations to former internees. Reparations for African Americans and Native Americans have also been debated, including Ta-Nehisi Coates' recent article "The Case for Reparations" concerning African Americans.

The malign actions committed against these groups by the government and European American citizens have been horrific. Forcible relocation in the case of Japanese and Native Americans. Wars of aggression against and theft of land from Native Americans. Slavery, Jim Crow, de facto slavery after the

Civil War, theft, unpunished murder, federal redlining of African American neighborhoods, and the mass incarceration of African Americans. The fruit of this oppression, in the case of African Americans, has been a huge wealth gap between African Americans and the rest of the country, as well as high incarceration rates.

Actions by the U.S. government against would-be immigrants have also been devastating. Millions of individuals have been deported from the country over the years, leading to immiseration, family separation, and sometimes death. (While not strictly a case of deportation, 254 refugees from the ship *St. Louis*, which was denied entry into the U.S. in 1939, died in the Holocaust. More recently, a man deported in 2012 to El Salvador, "dubbed by the United Nations as one of deadliest countries in the world," was murdered earlier this year by assassins hired by a disgruntled former tenant. A forthcoming study shows that close to one hundred deportees to Central American from the U.S. have been murdered over the last two years.) Moreover, hundreds of thousands of people have been detained each year and others harmed, even killed, by immigration agents. In addition, thousands have died in deserts trying to evade border enforcement along the southern U.S. border, while others have suffered abuse by non-government entities in transit to the U.S. or after arriving in the U.S. due to their undocumented status.

Furthermore, immigration restrictions on would-be immigrants have kept many in the developing world from escaping poverty. Restrictions prevent would-be immigrants from benefiting from the place premium, which allows a person from a disadvantaged country to earn much more in an advanced country, even without an increase in the person's skills. A paper by Michael Clemens and others concludes that "simply allowing labor mobility can reduce a given household's poverty to a much greater degree than most known antipoverty interventions inside developing countries." Restrictions also have blocked would-be immigrants access to a decent education in the U.S., which would increase their earnings potential.

In addition to locking would-be immigrants into poverty in the developing world, restrictions force them to work for low wages in dangerous conditions in sweatshops they would otherwise avoid by migrating. Some commentators have argued that having sweatshop jobs in poor countries is preferable to not having the jobs available at all (Nicholas Kristof: "… the central challenge in the poorest countries is not that sweatshops exploit too many people, but that they fail to exploit enough."). However, they fail to acknowledge that the fact that there are only these two alternatives is due to, as John Lee argued in a 2013 post on Bangladeshi sweatshop workers, "laws that ban Bangladeshis at gunpoint from working in our countries." John's post was published in the wake of a factory fire in Bangladesh that killed over 1,000 people, some of whom might have migrated to the U.S. under open borders rather than toiling in the unsafe factory.

Consider also women living in countries where they are mistreated who might escape to the freedom of the U.S. under open borders. It is difficult to determine the number of women who have been forced to endure misogyny in other countries because of restrictions, but it may be many.

The harm that our immigration laws have visited upon would-be immigrants is cumulative. They not only prevent today's would-be immigrants from improving their economic lives (not to mention that they kill and enable the abuse of some of them), they have been doing the same to their ancestors, leaving today's would-be immigrants much less well off than they might have been had their ancestors been able to migrate to the U.S. People in each generation who are barred from migrating are prevented from accumulating the wealth and educational capital to pass down to the next generation, and so on. The poverty one sees in developing countries is often largely the result of an inability of multiple generations to have accessed the advanced U.S. economy. This parallels the African-American predicament: An African American man told Mr. Coates that "The reason black people are so far behind now is not because of now… It's because of then."

The American government, and the people who have elected it, have caused immense harm, economic, physical, and psychological, to many immigrants over many years. Not only must we open our borders, some reparation is due to all immigrants. (Since most would-be immigrants have probably been negatively impacted by restrictions in some way, either directly or through their impact on their ancestors, reparations should be provided to all immigrants.) Determining the amount and nature of the reparation is complex, especially for those who have been killed or abused due to restrictions. As Mr. Coates suggests with regard to reparations for African Americans, "perhaps no number can fully capture the multi-century plunder of black people in America. Perhaps the number is so large that it can't be imagined, let alone calculated and dispensed."

Nonetheless, here are some ideas for reparations for immigrants under open borders. Part of a reparations package would be to grant immigrants immediate, full access to the American welfare state: Obamacare, Medicaid, Medicare, Social Security, TANF, job training, Pell Grants, federal student loans, housing assistance etc. For those concerned about elderly immigrants arriving to our shores and claiming benefits to which they have never contributed, remember that they would have happily contributed earlier had open borders been available when they were younger, and besides their personal finances have often been decimated for years due to immigration restrictions. With a center-left perspective, I believe some of these investments could reap later rewards, such as making it easier for new immigrants to attend college, which would in turn enhance productivity.

Moreover, new immigrants would be provided a set amount of money (maybe $5000), the services of cultural counselors and English teachers to help them get settled and oriented in the U.S., and low cost housing, services similarly provided for refugees today. These measures could smooth the country's transition to a significant increase in immigrants under open borders and bolster the economy by spurring construction of new housing and consumer spending. Finally, for those migrants who don't have resources to finance their travel to the U.S., travel assistance could be provided. (With regard to voting, I would continue to limit the franchise to those who have lived in the U.S.for a number of years to ensure that they fully understand the democratic foundation of our country before voting.)

Admittedly this all may be difficult for most people to accept: open borders and instant access to the welfare state, a cash allowance, low cost-housing, and travel assistance. Open borders plus reparations may not be popular even among many of my fellow open borders advocates. For example, it differs greatly from Nathan Smith's DRITI open borders plan, which burdens new immigrants with higher taxes than native-born Americans.

Mr. Coates has written about the deeper value of advocating for reparations (in the case of African Americans): "I believe that wrestling publicly with these questions matters as much as—if not more than—the specific answers that might be produced… An America that looks away is ignoring not just the sins of the past but the sins of the present and the certain sins of the future." Similarly, providing reparations for immigrants entering under open borders could eventually help instill the idea in Americans' hearts and minds that restrictions have constituted a great sin against a large portion of humanity, hopefully incubating Americans against reverting back to immigration restrictions.

Viewpoint 5

> *"Certainly, the blossoming of effective tribal self-government in the US is being eagerly watched by Indigenous peoples in other parts of the world, who are hoping to replicate this extraordinary success."*

Indigenous Reconciliation Fosters Healing

Sarah Maddison

The following viewpoint contrasts the U.S. and Canada's treatment of native peoples with that of Australia. According to the author, the U.S. has taken incomplete but important steps toward "reconciliation" with Native Americans, many of which have suffered extreme mistreatment in the past. These are steps that can be replicated in Australia with its Aboriginal population. For example, the U.S. Constitution recognizes tribal governments as "domestic dependent nations," each capable of varying degrees of autonomy. By contrast, no such recognition has been legislated in Australia. The author criticizes some aspects of U.S. policy, including the fact that the formal apology to Native Americans have never been real aloud by any public official. Finally, she advocates for Australia to build on these steps to enable Aboriginal self-determination. Sarah Maddison is associate professor at the School of Social and Political Sciences, University of Melbourne.

"Indigenous reconciliation in the US shows how sovereignty and constitutional recognition work together," Sarah Maddison, The Conversation, May 16, 2016. https://theconversation.com/indigenous-reconciliation-in-the-us-shows-how-sovereignty-and-constitutional-recognition-work-together-54554

As you read, consider the following questions:

1. How does the author characterize the difference between Australia and the U.S. with respect to each nation's treatment of native people?
2. Are the Native American nations true sovereign nations? What is the precise relationship between these groups and the U.S. government?
3. What are some shortcomings of Indigenous sovereignty?

Australia is being held back by its unresolved relationship with its Indigenous population. Drawing on attempts at reconciliation overseas, this series of articles explores different ways of addressing this unfinished business. Today, we turn to the United States to see how Native Americans fare.

Just like Australia's Aboriginal and Torres Strait Islander peoples, Native Americans have struggled for recognition of the violence done to them through colonisation and the persistent harms of settler colonialism. Recognition of this fact has given rise to various policies and programs that can be grouped together under the rubric of "reconciliation," whether or not they bear that label.

The key difference between Australia and the United States with regard to reconciliation rests on the recognition of Indigenous sovereignty. Treaties were negotiated with some hundreds of Native American tribes, and tribal sovereignty is recognised in the US Constitution.

Neither form of recognition exists in Australia. No treaties were negotiated with Aboriginal or Torres Strait Islander peoples. Debate about how they might be recognised in the Australian Constitution is ongoing.

Contemporary Native American nations, on the other hand, invoke their treaty relationships as an assertion of sovereignty that allows them to claim a "nation-to-nation" relationship with the federal government.

Despite significant shortcomings in the negotiation, content and subsequent honouring of treaties—and although the recognition of native sovereignty and treaty rights don't match the aspirations articulated by representative bodies, such as the National Congress of American Indians—treaties continue to define the nature of the relationship between most Native Americans and the US.

Definite Steps Forward

The power of native treaty rights is reinforced by the significant recognition of the nation-to-nation relationship between Indian tribes and the federal government contained in the US Constitution. Article 1, section 8, clause 3, which relates to the powers of Congress, says:

> The Congress shall have Power … To regulate Commerce with foreign Nations, and among the several States, and with the Indian Tribes.

This clause is widely interpreted as recognising a form of enduring sovereignty, given the other entities acknowledged in it are US states and foreign nations. And it has provided important benefits to many native peoples. It's evident, though, that there are differing levels of capacity to leverage these benefits among the 566 federally recognised tribes.

Despite continuing legal arguments about whether native nations should be understood as "domestic dependent nations", or part of a system of "constitutional trifederalism" (where tribes are understood as constitutionally recognised sovereigns, along with the states and federal government), there's little dispute that Indian tribes have a degree of legal recognition as sovereigns.

The existence of treaty relationships and constitutional recognition of tribal sovereignty are further buttressed by the 1975 Indian Self-Determination and Education Assistance Act. This allows the Bureau of Indian Affairs, the government department responsible for managing relationships with Native Nations, to contract services to the tribes themselves for implementation. The significance of this has been profound.

In the decades since 1975, many tribes have taken advantage of the self-determination policy to actually exercise sovereignty. Today, many control their own schools, health services and criminal justice systems.

Historian Charles F. Wilkinson argues that the "Indian revival" that's resulted should be regarded as comparable to the transformations of the civil rights era.

Certainly, the blossoming of effective tribal self-government in the US is being eagerly watched by Indigenous peoples in other parts of the world, who are hoping to replicate this extraordinary success.

And Some Steps Back

Despite these advances in political reconciliation between Native Nations and the US government, there's one area of the settler-Indigenous relationship where the US lags considerably.

Like Australia and Canada, the US subjected Native American people to the systematic removal of children from their families with the intention of eradicating their culture and inculcating them into settler ways of life. And, as in Canada, these children were primarily placed in boarding schools, where many suffered appalling abuses.

Also like both Australia and Canada, the US government has made a formal apology for these practices. But the Apology to Native Peoples of the United States has never been read aloud by any elected official.

Instead, it was signed into law by President Barack Obama, buried on page 45 of the 67-page Defense Appropriations Act 2010. The act is primarily concerned with the purchase of weapons and its signing was closed to the public. What's more, there was no official White House announcement about it.

In the absence of wider acknowledgement of the harms suffered during the time children were being separated from their families, the National Native American Boarding School Healing Coalition is leading calls for healing and reconciliation for survivors of the boarding school system.

This struggle, at least, is familiar to Australia.

But as the Harvard Project on American Indian Economic Development continues to document the successes of tribal governments, while Australian efforts to "close the gap" on Indigenous disadvantage deliver little good news, it's clear the pathway to meaningful reconciliation in Australia lies not in the continued paternalism of policies such as the Northern Territory Intervention (now known as Stronger Futures) but in political transformations that recognise enduring indigenous sovereignty and lead to genuine self-determination.

Periodical and Internet Sources Bibliography

The following articles have been selected to supplement the diverse views presented in this chapter.

Manuel Balce Ceneta, "Are Reparations Due to African-Americans?" *The New York Times,* June 8, 2014. http://www.nytimes.com/roomfordebate/2014/06/08/are-reparations-due-to-african-americans.

Maya Dania, "Former Sex Slaves Were Victims of War Crime," *The Jakarta Post,* January 1, 2016. http://www.nationmultimedia.com/opinion/Former-sex-slaves-were-victims-of-war-crime-30276980.html.

John Hawkins, "5 Reasons Reparations for Slavery Are a Bad Idea," *Townhall.com,* July 26, 2014. http://townhall.com/columnists/johnhawkins/2014/07/26/5-reasons-reparations-for-slavery-are-a-bad-idea-n1867139.

The House of Representatives, Text of Apologizing for the enslavement and racial segregation of African-Americans, June 29, 2008. https://www.govtrack.us/congress/bills/110/hres194/text.

Jean Paul Mugiraneza, "Rwanda Genocide: Why Compensation Would Help the Healing," *The Guardian*, March 4, 2014. https://www.theguardian.com/global-development-professionals-network/2014/mar/04/rwanda-genocide-victims-compensation.

The United Nations Statement to the Media by the United Nations' Working Group of Experts on People of African Descent, on the conclusion of its official visit to USA, January 2016. http://www.ohchr.org/EN/NewsEvents/Pages/DisplayNews.aspx?NewsID=17000&LangID=E#sthash.dBDDCQVX.dpuf.

Chapter 2

Does Implementation of Reparations Achieve a Satisfactory Solution?

Chapter Preface

Looking back over twentieth-century history, we can locate a few cases in which it became necessary to institute reparations. These are excellent case studies through which we may determine whether the specific reparation plans in question proved effective or not. In order to evaluate whether the outcomes of reparations are just and satisfactory, we must weigh the benefits that accrue to the recipient against whatever damage the burden of debt causes society at large. Obviously, too much debt can wreak economic havoc on a nation and lead to inflation and defaults. Moreover, the resulting debt spiral will likely exacerbate political, emotional, and psychological damage as well. In short, too onerous of an obligation to pay reparations can erode the morale of a country—including those collecting reparations. If the costs of reparations are too high, does this mean they should not be considered? Are there situations where reparations are inappropriate? Finally, can some forms of reparations purchase absolution for the aggressor at too cheap a price? We must consider these points to judge whether reparations are effective.

Historians point to interwar Germany as the prime example of a failed reparations plan. To punish Germany for its aggressive behavior in World War I, and also to finance war debts to the United States, the victorious allied nations of Europe levied heavy reparation costs on the defeated nation. Germany was unable to pay, precipitating a debt crisis. This paved the way for Hitler's rise to power, and eventually, World War II. Although the nations imposing reparations felt they were justified in seeking damages, the cure of reparations was ultimately worse than the disease.

Despite flawed implementation in the above case, reparations remain a viable concept for international disputes today. U.S. engagement in the Middle East, combined with new technologies of warfare such as drones, raise new questions about how to covertly compensate the officially unknown number of civilian casualties of foreign military operations. The U.S. military views these payments, which place a fairly cheap dollar value on human life, as a tool to win "hearts and minds." On the other side, some predict that violent non-state actors and terrorist groups with records of severe human rights abuses will eventually have to pay reparations to their victims as part of future negotiations.

Reparations can also be a gesture toward apology or reconciliation with a minority or aboriginal group within a wealthy powerful nation such as the U.S. or Australia. While these forms of reparation may appear too little too late to some, they can at least open a space for dialogue and healing. For this reason, opposition to such symbolic gestures lacks a credible basis.

Viewpoint 1

> *"Many agree that the economic crisis and the sense of national humiliation resulting from the unrealistic demands paved the way for Hitler to take over power and, eventually, led to the tragedy of World War II."*

Reparations Are Excessively Burdensome and Counterproductive

Boundless

In the following viewpoint, the author suggests that even when reparations are justified, too onerous of debt obligation can be problematic to the world economy. The article shows how heavy reparations were counterproductive to global stability in the aftermath of World War I, since Germany was unable to pay. Many at this time predicted that the national humiliation Germany experienced would have negative long-term consequences. Nonetheless, the victorious allied countries needed reparations to repay the United States. Without reparations, nations such as France and Italy had no hope of paying back their own debts. This led to a European debt crisis, one of the main factors leading to the Great Depression—and subsequently World War II.

"War Debts and Reparations," Boundless, May 20, 2016. https://www.boundless.com/u-s-history/textbooks/boundless-u-s-history-textbook/from-isolation-to-world-war-ii-1930-1945-26/non-interventionism-200/war-debts-and-reparations-1099-9740/.

As you read, consider the following questions:

1. What are some of the reasons why Germany had to pay heavy reparations after World War I?
2. Can you identify how the various reparations plans (Dawes Plan, Young Plan) differed?
3. How did the Great Depression exacerbate Germany's debt crisis and lead to fascism?

Reparations After World War I

World War I reparations were compensation imposed during the Paris Peace Conference upon the Central Powers following their defeat in World War I by the Allied and Associate Powers. Each of the defeated powers was required to make payments in either cash or kind. However, it was Germany that was officially held responsible for World War I and while other Allied powers' payments were soon dramatically reduced or cancelled, the 1919 Treaty of Versailles, which ended WWI, and the 1921 London Schedule of Payments required Germany to pay 132 billion gold marks (US$33 billion) in reparations to cover civilian damage caused during the war. Part of the sum was never expected from Germany and was included to deceive the Anglo-French public into believing Germany was being heavily fined and punished for the war.

An important factor that contributed to this development was a massive debt that American allies, most notably France and the United Kingdom, owed to the United States in the aftermath of World War I. As the United States demanded its debtors to repay their loans, both France and the United Kingdom hoped the post-war reparations from Germany to enable them to do so. A massive economic crisis that ensued in Germany as a result of these policies is considered to be the major factor in the eventual growth of Hitler's popularity and power.

Germany After World War I

Article 231 of the 1919 Treaty of Versailles (knows as the "War Guilt Clause") declared Germany responsible for all "loss and damage" experienced by the Allied and Associated powers during World War I. The Article noted that "Germany accepts the responsibility of Germany and her allies for causing all the loss and damage to which the Allied and Associated Governments and their nationals have been subjected as a consequence of the war imposed upon them by the aggression of Germany and her allies."

After negotiations, the 1921 London Schedule of Payments established the sum of 132 billion gold marks to be paid by Germany. This sum was a compromise promoted by Belgium against higher figures demanded by the French and Italians and the lower figure the British supported. It was divided into three series of bonds: "A" and "B" Bonds together had a nominal value of 50 billion gold marks (US$12.5 billion)—less than the sum Germany had previously offered to pay. "C" Bonds, comprising the remainder of the reparation figure, were included in the document to convince the public opinion that Germany was held fully responsible for the war but the Allied forced recognized that the German government would be unable to pay the sum. Taking into account the sum already paid between 1919 and 1921, Germany's immediate obligation was 41 billion gold marks. To pay towards this sum, Germany could pay in kind or in cash. Commodities paid in kind included coal, timber, chemical dyes, pharmaceuticals, livestock, agricultural machines, construction materials, and factory machinery. The gold value of these would be deducted from what Germany was required to pay.

Weimar Republic

Germans (between 1919 and 1933 referred to as Weimar Republic) viewed the Article 231 and the resulting reparations requirement as a national humiliation. German politicians were vocal in their opposition to the article in an attempt to generate international sympathy, while German historians worked to undermine the

"Comfort Women"

So-called "comfort women"—girls and women from countries Japan occupied in World War II—were forced by the Imperial Japanese Military to work as sex slaves for Japanese soldiers. Korean, Chinese, Filipina and other Southeast Asian women and girls were raped, forced into prostitution and sexual slavery. On Dec. 28, seven decades after the end of World War II, Japan and South Korea came to an agreement on compensating the surviving rape victims, but excluded them from contributing to the decision. The comfort women deserve so much more than this sham Agreement on the Military Sexual Slavery Issue.

The agreement reached by Prime Minister Abe and South Korea's President Park Geun-hye, designated final and irreversible by them, says that the Japanese government feels responsible for its military's committing sexual slavery and that Abe must apologize as Japan's representative. But the apology was made by a diplomatic representative, not Abe, who earlier had infuriated the comfort women by dismissing them as prostitutes.

South Korea will create a foundation to provide funding for the "comfort" women of $8.3 million in reparations from Japan. Once that funding is paid out by Japan, South Korea alone will run the foundation. The funds are for the care of the surviving victims of Japan's sexual slavery but, incredibly, none of the money will go directly to the victims.

The Agreement falls short. There are no preventive initiatives, including truth-seeking and the teaching of history. South Korea is even considering Japan's demand for the removal of the statue of the "comfort" woman in front of the Japanese Embassy in Seoul—supposedly to maintain the dignity of the Japanese Embassy. For the same reason, South Korea has agreed to limit its criticism against the government of Japan internationally.

Following are the, very principled, demands of the comfort women:

1. Full acknowledgment of the military sexual slavery implemented by the Imperial Armed Forces of Japan between 1932 and 1945.
2. Thorough and complete investigation to fully chronicle the scope of the crime.
3. Formal apology from the National Assembly (Diet) of Japan.

4. Legal and full reparations to all victims.
5. Prosecution of the criminals responsible for the crime.
6. Full and ongoing education through proper recording and acknowledgment in textbooks and history books in Japan.
7. Building of memorials and museums to commemorate the victims and preserve the history of sexual slavery by the Japanese Military.

While the U.S. government supports this Agreement in hopes that Japan and South Korea can counter-balance China, the surviving women and their supporters are more committed than ever to see that Japan actually be held responsible for its military sexual slavery.

"'Comfort' women dispute agreement," Elise, News and Letters Committees, January-February 2016 issue of *News & Letters*. http://newsandletters.org/comfort-women-dispute-agreement/. Licensed under CC BY ND SA 4.0 International.

article with the objective of subverting the entire treaty. The Allied leaders were surprised at the German reaction; they saw the article only as a necessary legal basis to extract compensation from Germany. American diplomat John Foster Dulles—one of the two authors of the Article—later regretted the wording used, believing it further aggravated the German people.

Under the burden of the reparation demands, the German economy was on the verge of collapse. As some of the payments were in industrial raw materials, German factories were unable to function, and the German economy suffered, further damaging the country's ability to pay. By late 1922, the German defaults on payments had grown so regular that a crisis engulfed the Reparations Commission; the French and Belgian delegates urged occupying the Ruhr, Germany's major industrial region, as a way of forcing Germany to pay more, while the British delegate urged a lowering of the payments. As a consequence of a German default on timber deliveries in December 1922, the Reparations Commission declared Germany in default, which led to the Franco-Belgian occupation of the Ruhr in January 1923. Particularly galling to the French was that the timber quota the Germans defaulted on was based on an assessment of their capacity the Germans made themselves and subsequently lowered. The entire conflict was further exacerbated by a German default on coal deliveries in early January 1923. The occupation, which led to the death of some German civilians, provoked pro-German sentiments within the international community.

The Dawes Plan and the Young Plan

The Allied occupation of the Ruhr industrial area contributed to the hyperinflation crisis in Germany, partially because of its disabling effect on the German economy. In response to the crisis, the Dawes Committee, chaired by Charles G. Dawes, proposed a plan in 1924. The Dawes Plan ended the occupation of the Ruhr region and reorganized German payments, which contributed to some level of stabilization of the German economy.

The Dawes Plan managed to end a major international crisis and Germany was able to meet its payment requirements. However, the plan was a temporary measure and in 1929, a new committee was formed to re-examine reparations. It was chaired by the American banker Owen D. Young and presented its findings in June 1929. The Young Plan was accepted and was ratified by the German Government in 1930. It established a theoretical final reparation figure at 112 billion gold marks (US300 million was to be raised and given to Germany.

The Great Depression

In March 1930, the German Government collapsed and was replaced by a new coalition led by Chancellor Heinrich Brüning. During 1931, a financial crisis began in Germany. In May, Creditanstalt—the largest bank in Austria—collapsed, sparking a banking crisis in Germany and Austria. In response, Brüning announced that Germany was suspending reparation payments. This resulted in a massive withdrawal of domestic and foreign funds from German banks. By mid-July, all German banks had closed. Until this point, France's policy had been to provide Germany with financial support to help Brüning's Government stabilize the country. Brüning, now under considerable political pressure from the far-right and President Paul von Hindenburg, was unable to make any concessions or reverse policy. As a result, Brüning was unable to borrow money from foreign or domestic sources. Further attempts to enlist British support to end reparations failed; the British said it was a joint issue with France and the United States. In early July, Brüning announced "his intention to seek the outright revision of the Young Plan." In light of the crisis and with the prospect of Germany being unable to repay her debts, United States President Herbert Hoover intervened. In June, Hoover publicly proposed a one-year moratorium to reparation and war debts. By July, the "Hoover Moratorium" had been accepted.

With the Great Depression now exerting its influence, the Bank for International Settlements reported that the Young Plan was unrealistic in light of the economic crisis and urged the world governments to reach a new settlement on the various debts they owed each other. During January 1932, Brüning said he would seek the complete cancellation of reparations. His position was supported by the British and Italians, and opposed by the French. Because of the political differences between countries on the subject and impending elections in France and Germany, a conference could not be established until June. This delay brought about the downfall of Brüning's Government. On 16 June, the Lausanne Conference opened. However, discussions were complicated by the ongoing World Disarmament Conference. At the latter conference, the US informed the British and French that they would not be allowed to default on their war debts. In turn, they recommended that war debts be tied into German reparation payments, to which the Germans objected. On 9 July, an agreement was reached and signed. The Lausanne Conference annulled the Young Plan and required Germany to pay a final, single installment of 3 billion marks, saving France from political humiliation and ending Germany's obligation to pay reparations.

The British economist John Maynard Keynes, in his best-selling 1919 book, argued that reparations threatened to destabilize the German economy and hence German politics. Keynes' views greatly influenced the way historians and economists assess the post-WWI reparations. Many agree that the economic crisis and the sense of national humiliation resulting from the unrealistic demands paved the way for Hitler to take over power and, eventually, led to the tragedy of World War II.

Viewpoint 2

> *"And just like governments, non-state armed groups such as IS and Boko Haram should provide reparations to their victims. It might seem like an impossibility now but it has happened before."*

Violent Non-state Entities Should Be Forced to Pay Reparations to Their Victims

Luke Moffett

In this viewpoint, Luke Moffett argues that non-state entities currently relying on violence to achieve their objectives may in the future be forced to provide reparations for their many victims. At the moment, it appears unlikely that the Islamic State or Boko Haram will compensate countless victims of kidnapping, torture, rape, and murder. However, Moffett uses the historical examples of FARC and the IRA to suggest that this could change, since both of those formerly violent groups are now actively involved in the peace process and have also provided some material compensation to victims as well. While military operations and criminal trials will be important in bringing leaders of these groups to justice, Moffett claims that reparations are the most direct way to alleviate the pain and suffering of those harmed by these groups. Luke Moffett is Law Lecturer in international criminal justice, Queen's University Belfast.

"Can Islamic State be forced to pay victims for their suffering?," Luke Moffett, The Conversation, November 19, 2014. http://theconversation.com/can-islamic-state-be-forced-to-pay-victims-for-their-suffering-34160.

As you read, consider the following questions:

1. What are some reasons why reparations are preferable to criminal trials, according to the author?
2. How could violent non-state groups operating "beyond the pale" ever be forced to pay reparations to their victims?
3. What are some other ways to provide justice for victims of groups like IS and Boko Haram?

The atrocities committed by Islamic State and Boko Haram have rightly caused moral outrage all over the world. But as the latest IS video is released, showing the faces of a group of IS militants, we might also start to think about the legal consequences of such outrages.

Air strikes have been mounted in Iraq in the hope of trying to stop the spread of IS and Nigerian troops have been deployed to battle Boko Haram, but little has been done to make reparations for the harm these groups have caused to ordinary people.

Both have kidnapped and murdered, and are responsible for the displacement of thousands of people. While air strikes and criminal trials may limit the violence, the victims remain without justice.

There have been calls for the International Criminal Court to investigate crimes by both groups but this would be difficult, given limits on the court's jurisdiction and its ability to protect witnesses.

Making Good

Reparations have been made by governments in the past when ordinary people have been victims of atrocities. The most famous case is probably the US$89 billion paid by the German government to Holocaust survivors.

Victims might get compensation, their property returned, medical help, apologies, acknowledgement of responsibility and guarantees that the crime won't be repeated. Reparations like these can in fact be a more effective form of accountability than criminal trials, although they generally need to be complemented by trials to ensure that they are not seen as simply buying off victims with "blood money."

And just like governments, non-state armed groups such as IS and Boko Haram should provide reparations to their victims. It might seem like an impossibility now but it has happened before. The IRA, for example, has played a part in peace building in Northern Ireland by providing information about people who were disappeared during the Troubles.

In Colombia the 2005 Peace and Justice Law required members of paramilitary groups to contribute their assets, including cars and holiday apartments in Belize, for reparations to victims. In return, their sentences were reduced. FARC has also proposed reparations to its victims as part of peace negotiations with the Colombian government.

IS and Boko Haram may seem beyond the pale, but for a long time FARC and the IRA were also terrorist groups with no political legitimacy. What happened later shows that non-state armed groups can be encouraged to engage with reparations to publicly acknowledge the harm they have caused and to alleviate the suffering of victims.

For the time being at least, IS and Boko Haram believe that their political goals are best achieved through violence. A day might come when they are forced to the negotiating table, at which point reparations could be suggested. And if they are not willing to hand over their money to victims or apologise creative tactics will be needed. That could mean seizing their assets in foreign countries or confiscating the resources of those companies that provide them with weapons, in the absence of political negotiation.

At the very least, if no resources or reparations are forthcoming from non-state armed groups, the state should ensure all individuals within its jurisdiction have access to an effective remedy, including reparations. While it may seem unfair that the state should be responsible for redressing the harm caused by groups outside its control, the needs of the people harmed by massacres and executions should be paramount.

The International Criminal Court has its own Trust Fund for Victims to provide interim assistance to victims of international crimes and it may be worth replicating such a system for the victims of IS and Boko Haram to help them, at least in the short term.

Military strikes are important to protect civilian populations, and criminal prosecutions are vital to tackle senior perpetrators. But reparations are how tangible justice is delivered to victims.

The young girls kidnapped by Boko Haram, the Yazidis forced from their homes by IS and the families of all the people murdered along the way will need all kinds of help if they are to rebuild their lives. Engaging non-state armed groups is not easy, but history tells us it is possible. We should not forget to remedy the suffering of victims who are left with the scars, trauma and poverty of violence [from] such groups.

Viewpoint 3

> *"The story of the Stolen Generations (Aboriginal) is not simply history. It is not something in the past that we need to get over."*

Apology-based Reparations Signal Empathy Not Responsibility

Nellie Green

Sometimes reparations are an apology, not material compensation. As Nellie Green explains in this viewpoint, the Australian government's practice of forcibly removing Aboriginal children yielded so-called "Stolen Generations." This is the name given to children who were taken from their families and placed in the care of white homes under the auspices of protection. While it is rarely spoken of outside of Australia, Green notes that this practice persisted until as recently as the 1970s. As a move toward reconciliation, Australia has instituted National Sorry Day, which Green believes is a positive development. She explains that even though those saying sorry were not directly responsible for racist policies of the past, the act of apologizing emphasizes solidarity and empathy. Nellie Green is Manager of Indigenous Student Services at La Trobe University.

"'Sorry' isn't the hardest word, so say it for the Stolen Generations," Nellie Green, The Conversation, May 25, 2012. https://theconversation.com/sorry-isnt-the-hardest-word-so-say-it-for-the-stolen-generations-7079.

As you read, consider the following questions:

1. Who are Australia's "Stolen Generations" and why did this phenomenon exist?
2. How does the author see her personal narrative relating to this unfortunate history?
3. Beyond being recipients of apologies, how does the author see Indigenous people fitting into contemporary Australian society?

As we are about to mark the 14th National Sorry Day and the fourth since the National Apology was delivered by former prime minister Kevin Rudd, I can't help but wonder if much has changed since the days when Aboriginal families such as mine had our children forcibly removed.

For many Aboriginal people, their lives are still controlled by government and various authorities, just like they were in the early days.

The Racial Discrimination Act was suspended to enable the Northern Territory Emergency Response (aka "The Intervention") to be enforced by the Liberal government, and the succeeding Labor government has extended its implementation, in my opinion, to the detriment of those Aboriginal people and communities it affects.

But all that is on a national level. Personally, I believe we are all connected by a common thread—some of us recognise this and others don't. Some of us acknowledge that the pain of others is the distress of all, just as the happiness or contentment of others can be our own satisfaction.

I like to share my experiences as an Indigenous person. Some people find my stories about stolen family members distressing, confronting, challenging. I choose to tell them.

I am not one for tokenism—especially when I am asked to talk about identity, the Stolen Generations and Sorry Day. I have often been asked by students, "But why should I say sorry? I wasn't there. I personally didn't do anything."

My response goes something like this: "When someone dies, we go to a funeral, we mourn the passing of a fellow human being who had a place in this world, and we tell their loved ones we are sorry for their loss. This 'sorriness' does not imply responsibility, but it extends remorse that someone is experiencing grief and loss."

It is not hard to understand really. The other thing I like to point out about Sorry Day and the Stolen Generations is that it is not an event buried in history.

Removal of children happened as recently as the early 70s.

In my family alone, I have seven cousins who were, at different times during the 1950s and 1960s, removed from their family, culture and country, including one cousin who was brought up and lives in Holland.

My mother's parents were both placed at Moore River Native Settlement, just north of Perth—even though they both had one white parent. My great-grandmothers were not suitable parents according to the "Chief Protector of Aborigines" in WA. Ironic, considering many Aboriginal women who had their own children forcibly removed were often placed with white families, their main responsibility being to look after the children.

Every birthday my own mother has is another year that marks the day her son was removed. For years, we couldn't understand why Mum didn't like a fuss on her birthday. We later discovered it was because it was also her son's birthday, and she had no idea what happened to him; no idea where he was.

We finally found out that my brother was adopted by a family from England. He and another Aboriginal boy were not only taken from their families; they were taken from their country, taken half-way around the world to be raised in Stockport.

I took that journey in 1992 to meet my brother, in Preston in the UK. Wow. My brother looks Aboriginal, but sounds like one of the Beatles.

All this happened five years before anyone had heard much of the "Stolen Generations," years before the Bringing Them Home Report was received by parliament in 1997.

I was later to discover that I had another older sister. That made three sisters instead of two, and two brothers instead of one. My sister was brought up here in rural Victoria with a white family, and also with an Aboriginal brother.

I am so grateful that they each had an Aboriginal sibling to grow up with. We met in 1999 and are very close, but it's inevitable you get to thinking about what's been missed over those years.

The story of the Stolen Generations is not simply history. It is not something in the past that we "need to get over." The time lost between family members is something that can never be replaced.

Personally, the lead up to Sorry Day is fraught with emotion and anxiety. I can only recall how it was to think I was one of four children, only to discover when I was 21 that I was actually one of six.

I never grew up with my big brother, because my big brother was not there. I never grew up with my second-eldest sister, because my second-eldest sister was not there.

My story is just one of many. Our stories can reach into people's hearts, they can remind people of things they might take for granted, and they can influence the way we might go about addressing some of things that cause disadvantage and exclusion.

This is particularly so in relation to Indigenous people accessing education and educating others about the experiences, aspirations and realities of Indigenous peoples.

I suppose at a local level and personally, I can say I have space for hope working at a university. I am committed to taking on the next stage of our journey through simple communication, genuine engagement, and the awareness that Indigenous students and staff are more than worth the investment.

Viewpoint 4

> *"Condolence payments came to be seen as a key part of the battle for 'hearts and minds' in Iraq and Afghanistan. But their implementation began slowly, and was marred by inconsistency."*

Condolence Payments Are Politically Expedient but Imperfect

Cora Currier

In the following viewpoint, Cora Currier outlines the U.S. military's practice of distributing condolence payments to civilian casualties of war. What emerges is an ad hoc system of paying off victims lacking consistency and uniform standards. Furthermore, the purpose of these payments, which are often quite low, is to convince hearts and minds that U.S. occupation is a positive force. Some in the military have even claimed these are "public relations" payments. As high-tech war has ramped up to include top-secret drone strikes, transparency regarding civilian body counts is difficult to attain, making condolence payments even more problematic. It remains to be seen whether the U.S. will solve these problems in Iraq, Afghanistan, and beyond. Cora Currier was a reporting fellow at ProPublica and previously on the editorial staff of the New Yorker.

"Hearts, Minds and Dollars: Condolence Payments in the Drone Strike Age," Cora Currier, ProPublica, April 5, 2013. Reprinted by permission.

As you read, consider the following questions:

1. When did the U.S. begin the practice of condolence payments?
2. Does the article imply that the main purpose of condolence payments is to compensate victims, or is there another motive?
3. What are some of the problems that may prevent condolence payments from being distributed fairly?

The U.S. drone war remains cloaked in secrecy, and as a result, questions swirl around it. Who exactly can be targeted? When can a U.S. citizen be killed?

Another, perhaps less frequently asked question: What happens when innocent civilians are killed in drone strikes?

In February, during his confirmation process, CIA director John Brennan offered an unusually straightforward explanation: "Where possible, we also work with local governments to gather facts, and, if appropriate, provide condolence payments to families of those killed."

There's little documentation of where and how such payments are being made. The government has released almost no information on civilian casualties sustained in drone strikes conducted by the CIA and the military in Pakistan, Yemen and Somalia. Officials maintain they have been "in the single digits" in recent years, while independent researchers put the total for the past decade in the hundreds.

Certainly, though, drone strikes and condolence payments make for a striking match: The technological apex of war combined with an age-old method of compensating loss.

Such condolence payments featured prominently in the wars in Iraq and Afghanistan. They are now embraced by many military commanders and by human rights advocates, some of whom are pushing for a system to govern what had been an ad hoc practice for most of the 20th Century: recognizing the dignity of life, even during war, and even with what might seem like a mere token acknowledgement.

The History of Condolence Payments

Condolence payments may be rooted in ancient custom, but they are a relatively recent addition to the terms and conduct of modern warfare. Neither U.S. nor international humanitarian law requires them, and they aren't, in technical terms, an admission of wrongdoing.

In fact, the Army regulation on such payments (which are also called solatia) describes them as "an expression of sympathy toward a victim or his or her family," in keeping with local custom. According to Center for Civilians in Conflict, an advocacy organization, the U.S. tradition of such payments dates back to the Korean War.

Foreign civilians have long had some recourse for compensation through the Foreign Claims Act, which permitted payments for damages caused by U.S. troops.

But the law doesn't cover anything that happens during active combat—a significant exception in situations where U.S. troops are on the ground, intermingled with civilian populations. The line between combat and non-combat isn't always clear. And even when soldiers feel their actions were justified, it is often to their advantage to recognize the harm done.

"Under the law of war, you can kill civilians, as long as their deaths are proportional to immediate military gain," said Gary Solis, a professor at Georgetown Law. "But as a nation, we recognize it's important to gain the trust of the people. As the complexion of war has changed, the significance of these payments has too."

Condolence payments came to be seen as a key part of the battle for "hearts and minds" in Iraq and Afghanistan. But their implementation began slowly, and was marred by inconsistency. The U.S., after pressure from military lawyers and other advocates, allowed payments fairly early on in the Iraq War. But in Afghanistan, they were not approved until 2005.

"It wasn't always popular with the soldiers, who would say, 'We're at war,'" said retired General Arnold Gordon-Bray, who led the 2nd Brigade of the Army's 82nd Airborne Division in the first months of the invasion of Iraq. "But I would say, 'We are going to leave, and the only thing that's going to remain is the perception of America.'"

Gordon-Bray described scraping together cash for informal payments before they were officially approved, and before Congress funded a cache of spending money for condolences, humanitarian assistance, and other "goodwill" projects. (In Afghanistan, the military continues to distinguish between those congressionally funded "condolence payments" and "solatia," which come out of a unit's operating funds.)

Even once the payments were officially authorized, the policy for implementing them wasn't clear or standardized and not all units paid them. For the local Iraqi population, there was often a lack of awareness about such payments and confusion about how to receive them.

Gordon-Bray said his team sometimes sought out surviving family members after a death. Soldiers also left cards behind after operations explaining how families could make claims. Other times, the onus was on the victims to identify the unit that had caused the damage, to collect evidence, and to bring it to the military's attention.

A military lawyer who served early on in Iraq told Congress in 2009 he occasionally had to turn down claims for lack of funds. He also said "two Iraqis who suffered substantially the same harm in different areas of the city would be treated very differently depending on what office they went to inside Baghdad to file their claim. [The] lack of standard rules really caused a lot of heartache."

There is little public documentation of condolence payments, though some batches of claims have been released. The details in those claims are scant, but often revealing about the relationship between soldiers and civilians.

One record, obtained by the American Civil Liberties Union, authorizes $1000 for "a Solatia payment for a lady whose son was killed by coalition forces." He had been shot in downtown Kabul when troops fired to disperse a crowd. An email noted the mother had been given "a complete runaround" in tracking down compensation.

In 2006, soldiers fired on a taxi that did not slow down at a military checkpoint in Iraq, killing a woman inside. The military determined the checkpoint wasn't adequately marked, and her family received a large payment, of $7,500.

"It's hard to digest that the value of a human life is a few thousand dollars," said Gordon-Bray, the general in Iraq. "But you know that in their economic situation, it is the equivalent of much more, and you feel better."

Today in Afghanistan, according to a Pentagon spokesman, condolence payments can be up to $5,000 for a death or injury, or $5,000 for property damage. Greater amounts can be approved in certain cases. In fiscal year 2012, the U.S. made 219 payments, totaling $891,000, according to a spokesman for U.S. forces in Afghanistan. (Solatia are not included in those figures.)

"The people we meet don't talk about the money so much as how they felt when they shook someone's hand—the recognition," said Erica Gaston, a senior program officer for the United States Institute for Peace, who works on Afghanistan issues.

According to Gaston and other advocates, it wasn't until 2008 that payments became commonplace among U.S. and coalition troops in Afghanistan, as part of a new emphasis on counterinsurgency.

Marla Keenan, managing director of the Center for Civilians in Conflict, said that that year saw a "strategic shift to 'hearts and minds,' which started to change the way commanders viewed condolence payments. It was a tool they could use to deal with populations."

In 2007, General David Petraeus, then head of U.S. forces in Iraq, described the tactical element of condolence payments: "The quicker you can do it, the more responsive you can seem to be... the more concerned you are, the more valuable it is, and the more helpful it is to your operation."

General James Conway, of the Marine Corps, was a bit blunter: "It doesn't make anything right. It does make it a little better from a public relations perspective."

Despite this embrace by military commanders, the payment systems can still seem improvised and imperfect.

Sen. Patrick Leahy, D-Vt., has tried several times to create a permanent set of rules and dedicated source of funding for condolence payments.

"Senator Leahy believes we need legislation to authorize it which gives discretion to field commanders and includes guidelines so the wheel doesn't have to be reinvented every time the U.S. military is deployed in combat," said Tim Rieser, his foreign policy aide.

Beyond Afghanistan

Should condolence payments become more codified, it is unclear how many, if any of those rules and requirements would apply to the world of targeted killings off the traditional battlefield. To date, the U.S. has yet to acknowledge any particular instance where a civilian was killed as a consequence of a drone strike outside Afghanistan—let alone if that person's family was compensated.

Pentagon spokesman Bill Speaks said that "the Department of Defense has not made solatia payments" in Yemen or Somalia, where the U.S. has acknowledged military action. The CIA's drone strikes in Pakistan and Yemen remain officially secret.

Neither the White House nor the Pentagon would comment further on Brennan's statement about condolence payments. The CIA also declined to comment.

There are occasional reports of condolence payments in Yemen and Pakistan, but the U.S. role in those payments—if there was one—remains unclear.

First Person Account: Japanese Internment

Seventy years ago, US soldiers bearing bayoneted rifles came marching up to the front door of our family's home in Los Angeles, ordering us out. Our crime was looking like the people who had bombed Pearl Harbor a few months before. I'll never forget that day, nor the tears streaming down my mother's face as we were forcibly removed, herded off like animals, to a nearby race track. There, for weeks, we would live in a filthy horse stable while our "permanent" relocation camp was being constructed thousands of miles away in Arkansas, in a place called Rohwer. [...]

The tragedy of the internment of 120,000 Japanese Americans was not only that it was the greatest violation of our constitutional guarantees, but that it broke apart families and whole communities, and left scars that today remain unhealed, even after the government later apologised and issued reparations. It was almost a half-century too late. President Ronald Reagan only reluctantly signed the Civil Liberties Act of 1988. It expressed regret for the injustice and paid a token redress of $20,000 to those survivors still alive. My father had already passed away in 1979, never to know of the apology or receive the redress money. I donated the sum to the most fitting institution, the Japanese American National Museum, which tells the story of the experience of Americans of Japanese ancestry.

"We Japanese Americans must not forget our wartime internment," by George Takei, *The Guardian*, April 27, 2012. Copyright © 2016 Guardian News & Media Ltd. Reprinted by permission.

In Pakistan, officials paid roughly $3,000 to the families of more than 30 people killed in a March 2011 strike. Last September, after a drone strike in Yemen killed as many as 14 civilians, families of the victims blocked roads and demanded compensation. According to the Washington Post, the Yemeni government publicly apologized and offered "101 guns to tribal leaders in the area as a symbolic gesture." Al Qaeda in the Arabian Peninsula reportedly sent its own offers of condolence. (The embassies of Yemen and Pakistan did not respond to questions about condolence payments.)

In recent months several former military and diplomatic leaders have expressed concern about reliance on drones to target terror suspects, and potential "blowback" from the program. A focus on targeting militants overlooks broad resentment of U.S. military actions, they said, echoing the issue that strained U.S. missions in Iraq and Afghanistan.

The U.S. also sends vast amounts of aid and provides counterinsurgency training to countries where it is hunting Al Qaeda-linked militants. Foreign aid to Pakistan includes earmarks for assistance to civilians harmed by military operations. That's in part to acknowledge the impact of the U.S. presence in the region, said Rieser, Senator Leahy's aide.

"But of course there is a limit to what we can do in a country whose government with which we often disagree, in a remote and dangerous region where implementing any program is difficult," he said.

The Obama administration is reportedly planning to shift control of the targeted killing campaign to the military, which officials said could bring greater transparency and accountability (with a notable exception for strikes in Pakistan, which the CIA will continue to handle.) Brennan has also said recently the U.S. should "acknowledge it publicly" when civilians were killed.

The pace of drone strikes has dropped off drastically in recent months, with just two reported in Pakistan in the past month. How civilian deaths will be handled in a more transparent future remains to be seen.

"The U.S. could open up the ability to make these payments in any theater," said Keenan, of Civilians in Conflict. "But in order to do it effectively, the U.S. has to engage on the ground. The whole point is acknowledging the harm."

"Legally, Japan, as a state, has atoned for its militarist past on a state-to-state basis, although there remains the questioned legal liability of private claims."

Legal Reparations Insufficiently Settle Moral Debts to Neighboring Countries

Yuka Fujioka

In the following excerpted viewpoint, Yuka Fujioka traces the "history issue" of Japan's relatively lenient post-war reparations. According to the author, Japan only complied with the minimum legal requirements for reparations, while downplaying symbolic or cultural reparations. This failed to heal the damage they caused as wartime aggressors and created tension in the region that remains to this day. While reasons for this dynamic are complex, the article identifies that the United States' interest in arming Japan as a proxy power against Soviet communism led to lax and contradictory peace treaty requirements. Moreover, the continuity between pre- and post-war Japan perhaps did not symbolically atone for the country's past militarism in the eyes of its neighbors. Yuka Fujioka is a Ph.D. candidate at Kobe University, Japan.

"Japan's Postwar Settlement in U.S.-Japan Relations: Continuity of Prewar Ideology in Domestic Politics," Yuka Fujioka, Business and Public Administration Studies, 2006.

As you read, consider the following questions:

1. How did U.S. policy goals at the dawn of the Cold War influence Japan's reparation obligations?
2. What are some reasons why Japan did not have to pay onerous reparations, despite its highly aggressive actions during the war?
3. How was the pre-war legacy preserved in post-war Japan, and why did this cause the appearance of insufficient atonement for war?

U.S. Postwar Settlement of Japan in the Cold War

In the introduction, I argued that Japan atoned legally as a state within the legal framework that was formulated to serve the strategic interest of the United States vis-à-vis communism in the postwar international environment. First of all, as far as the Tokyo trials are concerned, they were greatly influenced by the geopolitical interests of the United States, largely because the United States was virtually in charge of the Allied Forces occupation policies in Japan. The selection of judges was not impartial in a sense that there were only three Asians among eleven judges, in spite of the fact that Asian countries suffered the most serious damages by the Japanese Imperial Army during the Second World War.

Furthermore, the selection of defendants was deeply distorted. For instance, it has been recently revealed that General Douglas MacArthur granted an exemption from war responsibility to members of the 731 unit, a secret military medical unit of the Imperial Japanese Army headed by Ishii Shiro, a lieutenant general, who researched germ warfare in China through human experimentation, in exchange for the submission of their research data to the U.S. occupation forces.

Moreover, despite the criticism from other countries of the Allied Forces such as the Russians and the British, MacArthur sought to immunize Emperor Hirohito from war responsibility. From his successful experience with the psychological warfare against the Japanese in the Philippines, MacArthur knew the profound presence of the emperor in the minds of the Japanese. He wanted to retain the emperor to ensure peaceful control over the Japanese people in his occupation policy. Unless more official documents and information are disclosed by Japan's Imperial Household Agency and the Ministry of Foreign Affairs, it remains uncertain to what extent the emperor was involved in the process of the Japanese military expansion. In that sense, it would be premature to judge the emperor guilty at this point. However, at least, "MacArthur's truly extraordinary measures to save Hirohito from trial as a war criminal had a lasting and profoundly distorting impact on Japanese understanding of the lost war."[7] Because the Japanese people were indoctrinated to fight the war for the emperor, the fact that the emperor, the central cause for whom they fought the war, was not indicted and executed failed to completely convince them of their country's war guilt.

In addition, even Chiang Kai-shek opted not to indict the emperor in December 1945. "Faced with a civil war with the Chinese Communists, Chiang was afraid of Japan becoming communist if the indictment of the emperor and the abolishment of the emperor system took place."[8] Besides, by cooperating with the United States, he wanted to obtain the U.S. financial and military assistance and the use of surrendered Japanese military in China to fight against the Communists. In short, the advent of the Cold War greatly discouraged the extent to which the Allied Forces prosecuted Japan.

Besides, the start of the Cold War made the Tokyo trials different from the German trials. While the German tribunal took place before the Cold War, between November 20, 1945 and October 1, 1946, the Tokyo tribunal started in May 1946 and adjourned more than two years later in November, 1948 during which time the Cold War is thought to have started in early 1947. In other

7 Herbert P. Bix, *Hirohito and the Making of Modern Japan*, HarperCollins, New York, 2000, p. 585.

8 Awaya Kentaro, "Tokyo saiban ni miru sengoshori," in Yamaguchi Yasushi (ed.), *Sensosekinin, sengosekinin: Nihon to Doitsu ha dochigauka*, Asahi Shimbunsha, 1994, pp. 90-91.

words, "while the German trials were consistent and unaffected by the Cold War, the contradiction of the Tokyo trials further deepened, influenced by the Cold War between the US and the Soviet Union."[9]

In addition to the Tokyo trials, the U.S. occupation policy in Japan itself was reversed as the Cold War proceeded, and "by 1947, Japan had been replaced by a new American enemy, the Soviet Union."[10] As the only superpower immediately after the war, the United States had to restore the health of the world economy, for which "the new goal was the reconstruction and flourishing of the German and Japanese industrial economies as engines of world growth."[11] As a consequence, the grand purpose of the U.S. occupation policy towards Japan changed from democratization and demilitarization to economic reconstruction.[12] Moreover, the United States initially planned to rearm Japan by creating a Japanese army with some three hundred thousand men and in ten fully equipped combat divisions by 1953. The plan was not realized due to a strong opposition by Yoshida Shigeru, Japan's prime minister at the time. It was, however, a complete policy reversal compared to the Potsdam Declaration in July 1945 which banned Japan's rearmament in every way. This suggested plan of rearmament demonstrates how much the Cold War triggered the United States to be willing to reverse its occupation policy of Japan in such a short period after the war, despite the fact that militarism was one of major factors that caused Japan's acts of fanaticism before and during the war.

Even before the end of the Second World War by 1944, proposals to have Japan "integrated into a U.S.-created system"[13] became the basis of the U.S. postwar occupation policies. This was mainly because Chiang Kai-shek's regime, for the purpose of keeping his

9 Yamaguchi Tsutomu, "Futatsuno gendaishi" in Yamguchi Tsutomu (ed.), *Sensosekinin, sengosekinin*, Asahi Shimbunsha, Tokyo, 1994, p. 249.
10 Bruce Cummings, "Japan's Position in the World System" in Andrew Gordon (ed.), *Postwar Japan as History,* University of California Press, Berkeley, 1993, p. 36.
11 Yamaguchi, "Futatsuno gendaishi", p. 37.
12 Remarks by Yang Daqing, in Washington DC, November 26, 2001.
13 LaFeber, *The Clash*, p. 237.

armies intact for a future war against the Communists, became uncooperative to the United States by refusing to commit his troops in Burma and China. This led the United States to cease regarding China as a potential postwar policeman, when, to begin with, "[President] Roosevelt did not at all intend to turn Asia over to Chiang."[14] In addition, the Soviet Union was beginning to be viewed as a potential postwar threat against the United States.

Rescission of purging the Japanese war criminals detained at Sugamo Prison that accompanied the Tokyo trials also illustrated how the Allied Forces, namely the United States, reversed their occupation policy. As the Cold War intensified, the United States was beginning to lose the incentive of conducting the trials further. In order to ensure that Japan would not become communist, the General Headquarters/Supreme Commander for the Allied Powers in Tokyo reversed their policy from weakening old conservatives to nurturing anti-communist political power in Japan. As a result, many class-A war criminals including Kishi Nobusuke, Shigemitsu Mamoru and Sasagawa Ryoichi not only were released from prison but were allowed to climb up the social ladder again as prominent figures in politics and business. In fact, "forty-two percent of those elected to the lower house in October 1952, six months after the [San Francisco Peace] treaty came into force, were former purgees."[15] This created the continuity of the prewar ideology in Japanese politics, which will be explained more in detail later. Accordingly, "Defendants who had been convicted and sentenced to imprisonment became openly regarded as victims rather than victimizers."[16] In other words, "the Tokyo trials and the purges that accompanied them failed to solve the many-sided problem of war responsibility."[17]

Meanwhile, the U.S. softening policy towards defeated Japan was incorporated into the 1951 San Francisco Peace Treaty. To

14 LaFeber, *The Clash*, p. 231.

15 Richard B. Finn, *Winners in Peace: MacArthur, Yoshida, and Postwar Japan*, University of California Press, California, 1992, p. 296.

16 John W. Dower, *Embracing Defeat: Japan in the Wake of World War II*, W.W.Norton & Company / The New Press, New York, 1999, p. 513.

17 Bix, *Hirohito and the Making of Modern Japan*.

begin with, among forty eight signatories, neither Communist China in Beijing nor Nationalists in Taiwan, who received the most severe damage during the war by the Japanese, were invited. Reflecting an increasingly intense confrontation between the East and the West, "the Peace Treaty turned out to be one sided"[18] in a sense that it concluded peace with "countries excluding those in the Eastern bloc under the Cold War structure."[19] Yugoslavia, India and Burma rejected their participation, although they were invited. The Soviet Union, Poland and the Czech Republic participated but refused to sign, opposing the contents of the Treaty.

It has been pointed out by many historians that it was a generous and non-punitive treaty, because "with the consideration by the United States and Great Britain, the reparation clause was softened."[20] Article 14 (a) of the Treaty states that "it is recognized that the resources of Japan are not presently sufficient, if it is to maintain a viable economy, to make complete reparation for all such damage and suffering and at the same time meets its other obligations."[21] In short, it allowed Japan to pay reparations according to its economic capabilities at the time and in the form of goods and services of the Japanese people in production, rather than financial reparation. It also allowed Japan to negotiate with victimized countries to decide the total amount of reparations and contents instead of unilateral decisions of reparation by the allied countries.

Such moderate reparation treatment was partly because John Foster Dulles who was charged with negotiating the Treaty believed at an early stage of the Treaty formation that severe punishment would be counterproductive in the long run. Such belief was based upon a widely recognized theory and his own belief that harsh terms imposed upon Germany at the Treaty of Versailles after World War I caused the later collapse of their economy and the rise of fascism (Nazism) in Germany. At the same time, this

18 Yoshida Yutaka, *Nihonjin no sensokan*, Iwanami Shoten, Tokyo, 1995, p. 68.

19 Iokibe Makoto, *Nichibei senso to sengo Nihon*, Osaka Shoseki, Osaka, 1989, p. 204.

20 Nagano Shinichiro and Kondo Masaomi, *Nihon no sengobaisho*, Keiso Shobo, Tokyo, 1999, p. 4.

21 Excerpts from Article 14 (a) in Treaty of Peace with Japan, September 8, 1951.

softened reparation policy stemmed from the new geopolitical reality based on which "U.S. officials regarded Japan's allegiance in the Cold War as absolutely essential, for without Japan, it was argued then, the 'global balance of power' would shift in favor of the Soviet Union."[22] In fact, it was a generous treaty compared with the Peace Treaty with Italy, another Axis country, because the Italian Peace Treaty was punitive overall in every aspect. For instance, it demanded a specific amount of financial payment as reparations (the total of 360 million dollars),[23] while the San Francisco Peace Treaty allowed Japan and Allied Powers whose territories were damaged by Japan to negotiate contents of compensations.

In the end, with strong pressure from the United States that advocated a non reparation policy for Japan, most allies relinquished reparation rights. As a result, the only reparation that Japan paid was to four countries, including the Philippines in 1956, Indonesia in 1958, Burma in 1954 and South Vietnam in 1959, in the form of goods and services spread out over many years. Other Asian countries including Cambodia, Laos, Malaysia, Singapore, Thailand and North Vietnam decided to make an economic cooperation agreement with Japan, instead of claiming reparations. It is a well known fact that these capital transfers to countries in Asia in the form of economic cooperation eventually helped the rise of the East Asia economy, which in turn provided Japanese companies with manufacturing bases. With regards to Korea which was seriously damaged by Japan, Japan eventually provided South Korea an economic aid package as grants and "loans." As for China, Zhou Enlai, the country's premier then, agreed to surrender all claims to war reparations from Japan in the context of its normalization of diplomatic relations with Japan in 1972, and Japan agreed to provide official development assistance (ODA) to China, both in grant and "yen loans." Komori Yoshihisa, a prominent Japanese journalist, argued that it should be helpful for South Korea and China to have been provided with low interest loans.[24] However, I would argue

22 John W. Dower, "Yoshida in the Scales of History" in John W. Dower (ed.), *Japan in War and Peace: Selected Essays*, The New Press, New York, 1993, p. 230.
23 Toyoshita Narahiko, *Anpojyoyaku no seiritsu*, Iwanami Shinsho, Tokyo, 1996, p. 231.

that, as alternative means to wartime reparations,[25] provisions of economic aid as "loans" would not send a message of apology and repentance from China's perspective, particularly because unlike other victimized countries in Asia, it generously gave up the claim for war time reparations. Sincere apology must not accompany mercantile calculations.

Yoshida Shigeru, Japan's prime minister in 1951, seemed to have been reluctant to attend the Peace Conference in San Francisco, not because he was opposed to the Peace Treaty itself but because he was opposed to the bilateral U.S.-Japan security treaty which the United States made an absolute condition for Japan to sign concurrently in order to obtain the country's sovereignty through the Peace Treaty. It was an inequitable security treaty that subordinated Japan. In reality, the primary purpose of the security treaty was to project U.S. power in Asia all the way to the Middle East by allowing the United States to station its troops in bases in Japan including Okinawa. Although the Treaty stated "to deter armed attack upon Japan"[26] by external threats, in fact, by allowing the U.S. troops to station in bases in Japan, Japan would have had to face external threats such as the Soviet Union, which it would not have had to face without the presence of the U.S. troops.[27] "It integrated Japan into the anticommunist camp and simultaneously created a permanent structure of U.S. control over Japan."[28] In short, Yoshida knew that Japan would gain independence and softened wartime reparation treatment by the Peace Treaty but at the same time would face subordination by the Security Treaty.

24 Remarks made by Komori Yoshihisa, Senior Editor, Sankei Shimbun, at Sigur Center for Asian Studies at George Washington University on December 5, 2001.

25 The Japanese government makes a distinction between wartime reparations and official development assistance (ODA), stating that ODA is not reparations.

26 Excerpt from Security Treaty Between the United States of America and Japan.

27 On this point, there exists a split of interpretations. For example, according to Iokibe Makoto, Yoshida well recognized that the presence of US troops in Japan, by concluding the US-Japan security treaty, was not the cost but vital importance for Japan's security from the Soviet Union. See Iokibe Makoto, *Senryoki: shusho tachino shinnippon*, Yomiuri Shimbunsha, Tokyo, 1997, p. 387.

28 John W. Dower, "Peace and Democracy in Two Systems: External Policy and Internal Conflict," in Andrew Gordon (ed.), *Postwar Japan as History*, University of California Press, Berkeley, 1993, p. 11.

Continuity of Prewar Ideology in Japanese Politics

So far, I have explained how the U.S. postwar settlement with Japan was reversed and softened in the face of the Cold War, how such policy failed to cleanse Japan's prewar ideology based upon the emperor system and, how it complicated the understanding by the Japanese people of their country's war responsibility as a wartime aggressor. In fact, the continuity of the prewar ideology and incomplete sense of guilt as an aggressor could be observed in many aspects of the postwar Japanese domestic politics. This was greatly because "Washington restored to power many of the old conservative guard who had guided Japan's imperial policies"[29] by releasing them from Sugamo Prison in Tokyo.[30]

For instance, the inauguration of Yoshida as prime minister is one evidence that the prewar ideology continued and was embraced in Japanese politics even during the postwar period. Yoshida is known as the most prominent political figure of the postwar period of Japan. With hindsight, he made an enormous contribution to Japan by laying the foundational direction for the country's postwar reconstruction and successful economic prosperity. Nevertheless, I would argue that he was a prewar politician who preserved the old ideology. The fact that someone like him who had "profound devotion to the emperor system" and whose "number-one priority in the aftermath of the war was the preservation of the emperor system"[31] became Japan's postwar prime minister right after the country's defeat in the war suggests that Japan did not fully learn a lesson. In fact, "Yoshida was ideologically opposed to virtually all basic reforms associated with the early Occupation 'democratization' agenda."[32] Moreover, although he was not imprisoned as a war criminal, he once served

29 Mike M. Mochizuki, *Japan Reorients: The Quest for Wealth and Security in East Asia*, Brookings Institution Press, Washington D.C., Forthcoming.

30 For example, between 1951 and 1952, about 200,000 former officers were de-purged. For more detailed accounts, see Michael Schaller, "Altered States: The United States and Japan Since the Occupation," Oxford University Press, New York, 1997, p. 38.

31 Dower, "Yoshida in the Scales of History," p. 218.

32 Dower, "Yoshida in the Scales of History," p. 224.

as the counsel general of hoten[33] in Manchuria and later as the vice minister of foreign affairs, and he played an active role in Japan's act of aggression in China. Furthermore, Yoshida, "without questions, had an obvious racial prejudice against people and countries in Asia."[34] For instance, Yoshida reveals his discriminatory view towards Asians, in his memoir, *Kaiso Junen*[35] in which he states that Japan which has been an independent state since the Meiji era and the rest of Asian states which newly became independent should be treated differently and that Asian states are with low cultural standards and remain in the stage of underdevelopment. And, Wakamiya Yoshibumi, a chief editor of Asahi Shimbun, argues that one should not ignore how much influence his racial prejudice against Asians had on postwar Japan because Yoshida is the one who laid the foundation of Japan's postwar politics.[36]

Another indication that proves "continuity of prewar and postwar politics"[37] in Japan is that Kishi Nobusuke, who was once a class-A war criminal, not only returned to the country's central political arena but also became prime minister in 1957. During the era of Japan's military aggression, he served as minister of commerce and industry and was a leading economic planner in the puppet state of Manchukuo in the 1930's. Under the Tojo Cabinet, he was a vice minister of munitions in 1943 and 1944. For these reasons, he was accused as a class-A war criminal and imprisoned at Sugamo Prison from late 1945 to 1948. However, with a drastic shift of the U.S. occupation policy, he was not only released without trial but was allowed to return to the political arena.

Kitaoka Shinichi points out two facts about Prime Minister Kishi as some evidence that Japan has apologized on numerous occasions:[38] 1) Prime Minister Kishi apologized for Japan's act of aggression during the war before the Australian parliament, and

33 Today's Shen Yang in Liaoning, China.
34 Wakamiya Yoshibumi, *Sengohoshu no ajiakan*, Asahi Shimbunsha, Tokyo, 1995, p. 57.
35 Yoshida Shigeru, *Kaiso Junen*, Shinchosha, Tokyo, 1957.
36 Wakamiya, *Sengohoshu no ajiakan*, p. 59.
37 Mochizuki, *Japan Reorients: The Quest for Wealth and Security in East Asia*, Forthcoming.
38 Kitaoka, "The Folly of the Fiftieth Anniversary Resolution."

2) he also sent a message of apology to President I Seung-man of South Korea shortly after taking office. On one hand, it is not a matter of objection or criticism and was in fact a legitimate act for the Japanese prime minister to express apology to victimized countries. That a straightforward apology was expressed by the Japanese prime minister to those victimized should be highly valued and it should be regarded as a case of evidence that Japan has apologized. It was foreseeable that members of the Australian parliament and the South Korean President at that time would accept Prime Minister Kishi's sincere apology "as an individual." On the other hand, however, it was highly plausible that they would have, at the same time, deeply questioned Japan's ability to repent its past guilt "as a country" which, to begin with, allowed someone like Kishi who was once a class-A war criminal to serve as the head of the state. The fact that a class-A war criminal served as prime minister clearly demonstrates that Japan did not embrace a strong sense of guilt and war responsibility. In this sense, Kitaoka Shinichi overlooked the negative image of Japan to the world caused by a former class-A war criminal serving as a head of the state, when viewed from the rest of the world, especially from victimized countries' perspective.

Among other examples that illustrate continuity of prewar and postwar politics, the fact that Hatoyama Ichiro became prime minister after Yoshida was equally problematic. He was also purged but had a record of having supported not only Japanese aggression in the Second World War but also the suppression of dissent in the 1920's and 1930's.

Shigemitsu Mamoru who became vice prime minister and foreign minister in 1954 in the Hatoyama Cabinet that succeeded the Yoshida Cabinet was also a class-A war criminal. He served as foreign minister under the Tojo Cabinet during the war and was sentenced to seven years' imprisonment after the war. Nevertheless, he was paroled with other class-A war criminals in 1950 without fully serving his sentence and returned to the public life, becoming party leader of Reform party and serving as foreign minister and vice prime minister afterwards. Moreover, he was awarded the First Order of Merit by Emperor Hirohito in 1957. In short, the fact that those who were once war criminals returned to the national politics and took up extremely important positions in the Diet "made Japan's war responsibility ambiguous all the more."[39]

There are many other examples in the Japanese central political arena that demonstrate the continuity of prewar ideology in the postwar politics up to the present. A series of remarks repeatedly made that deny Japan's acts of aggression during the war by the Cabinet members, including Fujio Masayuki[40] who was minister of Education in the Nakasone Cabinet until 1986, and Nagano Shigeto[41] who resigned his post as minister of Justice in the Hata Cabinet in 1994, are obvious ones. The quagmire at a time of the Murayama Cabinet in 1995 in formulating a "no-war" resolution to commemorate the fiftieth anniversary of the end of the Pacific War would be another. Besides, in 2000, former Prime Minister Mori made a controversial remark that Japan is *kaminokuni*, a divine nation with the emperor at its center, which is reminiscent of Japan's pre-World War II creed and violates the country's postwar constitution that states that sovereign power resides with the people. He also let it slip once that we needed to protect *kokutai*, national polity which is the structure of a state centering on the emperor. Furthermore, the current Prime Minister Koizumi has called some of the class-A war criminals buried at the Yasukuni Shrine "martyrs," and he keeps paying homage at the shrine in his official capacity even at the cost of further deteriorating the country's relations with China and South Korea. These remarks

39 Wakamiya, *Sengohoshu no ajiakan*, p. 49.
40 In an interview for *Bungei Shunju* in September 1986, he made controversial statements regarding Japan's role in World War II, claiming that "killing people in war is not murder in terms of international law" and that the Tokyo War Trial "cannot be considered correct." He also equated Japanese visiting Yasukuni Shrine as Chinese visiting Confucius temples, and argued that the Nanjing Massacre is a fabrication. He was promptly fired by prime minister Nakasone, as he refused to apologize and withdraw his statements.
41 In May 1994, he publicly stated that Japan did not invade Asia, the Rape of Nanjing was a fabrication, and that military comfort women were simply prostitutes. He once held his position as Army Chief of Staff.

are just representative of the idea that many political leaders still embrace the prewar ideology even at present and that they have not fully atoned psychologically apart from the country's official stance on Japan's militarist past.

In addition, one could observe other elements of the prewar ideology besides the emperor worship and justification of Japan's act of aggression that are preserved and exercised in Japan's postwar foreign policies. For instance, Ohira Masayoshi, who became prime minister after Tanaka Kakuei in late 1978, seemed to have still preserved Japan's prewar idea of the Greater East Asia Co-Prosperity Sphere. In the course of drastically increasing trade with China after signing a Treaty of Peace and Friendship in 1978, Ohira began to advocate a "Pacific rim strategy to integrate China and Southeast Asia's raw materials and markets into Japanese capital and technology."[42] This is slightly different in a sense that before the war, Japan did not have capital and technology and attempted to exploit natural resources by force. But, the idea seems similar in a sense that Japan attempted to take a hegemonic role in Asia, this time in terms of economic integration. In fact, Japan gradually pursued this foreign economic policy, this time not by military might but by economic might.

Ohira also pursued a defense policy that reflected the prewar ideology that caused the war. Proposing a military policy, "Comprehensive National Security," the Ohira Cabinet sought to "include more cooperation with Western militaries, to raise Japan's military profile."[43] A report made by Japan's Defense Agency in July 1980 "noted the termination of clear American supremacy in both military and economic spheres" and "urged building up Japan's defenses, especially to secure oil supplies."[44] The period of the Ohira Cabinet as well as the period of Tanaka Kakuei and Fukuda Takeo as prime ministers from the early 1970's coincided with Japan's drastic increase of economic power. From this perspective, it appeared a reasonable want for the country to attain a more

42 LaFeber, *The Clash*, p. 369.
43 LaFeber, *The Clash*, p. 370.
44 LaFeber, *The Clash*, p. 370.

independent defense policy commensurate with its economic power. In particular, Japan has always been dependent upon the United States in defense under the U.S.-Japan security treaty since it was signed in 1951, and the country has never been able to formulate a fully independent defense policy.[45] However, one could observe, in the report, the revival of the prewar idea, "building up defenses to secure oil supplies," that led the country to a quagmire of war. It would not have been unreasonable for observers to argue that Japan has not fully learned a lesson from its militarist past after more than fifty years since its defeat in the war.

Another element of the prewar ideology is Japan's racial prejudice against other countries in Asia.[46] This could be observed in remarks made by Nakasone Yasuhiro who was prime minister in 1980's. For example, he wrote in 1978 about "a new civilization that would integrate less developed countries under Japan's guidance."[47] One cannot fully ascertain his discriminatory ideology against countries in Asia only from this remark, but one could at least sense the prewar idea preserved in his mind that Japan would guide the rest of Asia as a hegemon.

One could observe from the examples above that postwar major political leaders of the Liberal Democratic Party (LDP), whose mainstream political philosophy is derived from that of Yoshida, did not cleanse but retained the prewar ideology that caused the war of aggression, without going through full psychological atonement. And, to begin with, it was originally the United States, with its newly formed geopolitical interest under the emerging Cold War international structure, that allowed those prewar conservative elites to return to Japan's central political arena.

45 On this point, there is a debate over whether Japan did not have autonomy over its postwar defense policy or it actually chose to depend on the United States in defense in spite of having a high degree of control over its defense policy. For a view that supports postwar Japan having maintained its autonomy, see Mike M. Mochizuki, "U.S.-Japan Relations in the Asia-Pacific Region" in Iriye Akira and Robert Wampler, (eds.), *Partnership: The United States and Japan, 1951-2001*, Kodansha International, Tokyo, 2001, pp.13-32.

46 On this point, John W. Dower described extensively in *War without Mercy: Race and Power in The Pacific War*, Pantheon Books, New York, 1986.

47 LaFeber, *The Clash*, p. 373.

With hindsight, the LDP leadership greatly contributed to Japan's postwar reconstruction and subsequent economic prosperity. And yet, because the LDP dominated Japanese politics since 1955 for half a century up to the present, it would not be an exaggeration to say that the Japanese public, in one way or another, has been psychologically influenced by the prewar ideology through the LDP politics.

Postwar Japan succeeded in attaining its economic prosperity, yet at the cost of suffering from the "history issue" that haunts its diplomacy in the long run.

Periodical and Internet Sources Bibliography

The following articles have been selected to supplement the diverse views presented in this chapter.

Olivia Lang, "Why has Germany taken so long to pay off its WW1 debt?" *BBC News*, October 2, 2010. http://www.bbc.com/news/world-europe-11442892.

Barbara Mcmahon, "Tasmania to pay 'stolen generation' of Aborigines £2.2m in reparations," *The Guardian*, January 23, 2008. https://www.theguardian.com/world/2008/jan/23/australia.international.

Bilal Qureshi, "From Wrong to Right," NPR, August 9, 2013. http://www.npr.org/sections/codeswitch/2013/08/09/210138278/japanese-internment-redress.

Aylssa Rosenberg, "Japan, World War II and the case for reparations in the United States," *The Washington Post*, July 28, 2014. https://www.washingtonpost.com/news/act-four/wp/2014/07/28/japan-world-war-ii-and-the-case-for-reparations-in-the-united-states.

Liam Stack, "After Airstrike on Afghan Hospital, a Look at U.S. 'Condolence Payments,'" *The New York Times*, October 11, 2015. http://www.nytimes.com/interactive/2015/10/11/world/us-condolence-payments.html?_r=0.

Chapter 3

What Form Should Reparations Take?

Chapter Preface

Frustrated by opposition from those who would deny, obfuscate, or underestimate systemic racism in present-day America and its continuity with slavery and segregation, some activists are developing new practices for reparations. By focusing on the redress of collective rather than individual wrongs, these advocates sidestep by-now familiar objections to taxpayer-funded reparation plans: that they penalize the blameless for sins committed by the long-deceased. By contrast, the funding of scholarships through wealth amassed by corporations with direct ties to slavery is likely to appear much more fair to average Americans.

Building on the above, other thinkers and activists are taking a more radical approach to the question of reparations, deconstructing the very notions of credit and debt informing the concept and process. Thus, rather than keeping a balance sheet of rights and wrongs, subscribers to this viewpoint might instead look at how we exist in an interconnected social world that is governed by more than simple material exchange. Naturally, such a framework provides little specifics by way of material compensation. However, it may help us rethink the ultimate purpose of reparations, especially when dealing with complex historical systems of exploitation such as slavery and colonialism–systems with lingering destructive effects to the present day.

An understanding of reparations that transcends credit, debt, and other concepts linked to capitalism can illuminate why some parties such as Native Americans choose to opt out of reparations. The refusal of reparations accomplishes two things. Within the framework of exchange, it refuses to give up bargaining leverage by taking a bad deal. And perhaps more important, such a move subverts the underlying logic of commodification and exchange. In the case of those with radically different understandings of humans' relationship to land and the natural world, such a refusal is not only good business, it is also a response to those that would threaten their culture and way of life existentially.

VIEWPOINT 1

> *"Extreme wrongs require extreme remedies."*

Reparations Would Remedy White Supremacy in America

David Schraub

In this viewpoint, David Schraub clarifies many of the conceptual errors and logical fallacies cited by opponents of reparations. Foremost, Schraub takes issue with those who oppose reparations based on irrelevant assignations of historical blame. Such arguments, he asserts, miss the point. Instead, the author supports programs such as one advanced by the NAACP to create scholarships for minorities funded by corporations with historical ties to slavery. Such programs shift the focus of the debate away from righting wrongs that can never be undone toward pragmatic ways to solve inequities in the present world. David Schraub is assistant editor at the Moderate Voice.

As you read, consider the following questions:

1. How does the author refute arguments against reparations?
2. Does the author feel that too much time has passed to consider reparations?
3. How might the "backlash theory" play out, according to those against reparations?

"They're Boycotting What? And Other Thoughts on Reparations," David Schraub, The Moderate Voice, July 14, 2005. http://themoderatevoice.com/theyre-boycotting-what-and-other-thoughts-on-reparations.

In a prior post, Joe notes the revival of slave reparations by American companies. Though these aren't your stereotypical reparations—they're offering scholarships and education funds, not blanket checks—TMV still believes that any effort by groups like the NAACP to boycott companies who refuse to pay will be met by "a boycott by a counter group (or two) to get businesses not to participate."

I don't think that will happen, especially since the reparations are not in the form of plain cash. It's easy for commentators to grumble about reparations in the abstract. They can recite tired old arguments like "it assigns blame to innocent parties" and "it isn't what we should focus on today" (see below for more). But opposing a real-life policy of scholarship funds for minorities–and taking it to the extreme of boycotting companies that provide them? I'm cynical about racial relations in America, and I can't imagine any group stupid enough to invite that much bad press. Because, let's be honest—they're boycotting a company because said company is giving scholarships to blacks. That's how it will be reported in the media, and that's how the casual American will see it. Gee, how could that ever be taken the wrong way?

Of course, the issue of reparations as a normative matter is entirely separate. Yet, after a fair bit of the thought on the issue, I've concluded that reparations are a moral obligation for a country which too long has shirked it's obligations to remedy systematic white supremacy, both past (de jure) and present (de facto). Larry Bernard argues that reparations are wrong because

> Reparations ignores [sic] the fact that the US government/ Colonial government was a force that freed many slaves.
>
> The role of abolitionists to the freedom of slaves.
>
> The role of Africans in selling them into slavery.

Determining Who Qualifies for Reparations

Under today's racial preference rules, a nephew of the King of Spain or the daughter of the chairman of the biggest bank in Chile would both qualify for Hispanic preferences if they resided in the United States. Harvard can (and does) meet its African American diversity requirements with the children of recent African immigrants, whose families never experienced slavery or segregation in this country.

The problem of "who qualifies?" is explosive enough with hiring and admissions preferences. As the benefits at stake expand to the vast dimensions urged by Coates, the question will become more explosive yet. Does a mixed race person qualify? How mixed? What about recent immigrants from Africa or the West Indies? What about future immigrants? What about illegal immigrants from Africa who subsequently gain legalization—would amnesty come with a check attached?

"The Impossibility of Reparations," David Frum, *The Atlantic*, June 3, 2014.

The blame can go back to multiple countries that don't even have the capacity to pay for reparations.

Arguments which, themselves, miss the point. First of all, Bernard's history is way too rosy. In some cases at some times, the US government was a force for abolition. At other times, it was a force for enslavement. For the vast majority of the time (at least up until *Brown* in 1954), American governments were nearly universally a force for racial subordination, slavery or no. I think it's historically undeniable that America, as a nation, is still well in the negative in terms of its racial debts—a fact that exists independent of whatever blame specific African tribes had in the slave trade (this issue is also severable—as Bernard admits, most African nations couldn't even afford to pay reparations, so that "solution" is inapplicable. But while they can't, we can). But even if you don't believe that, the narrative he tells has absolutely nothing to do with corporations that benefited from slavery, which is where the NAACP is pressing the issue.

Second, Bernard mentions the role of abolitionists in freeing the slaves. I do not deny their role, but I question the relevancy to the debate at hand. The implicit argument Bernard is making is that "reparations damage white people, which is unfair because not only is it untrue that all whites were slave owners, but some whites affirmatively opposed slavery." The problem is twofold. First, again, the NAACP is specifically focusing on companies which benefited from slavery—not whites in general. Second and more importantly, however, it misconstrues the purpose of reparations. It isn't to "get back at Whitey." Rather, it is to remedy inadequacies and inequalities that have resulted from the slave system—inequalities in which all whites benefit. In a system which structurally advantages whites, all whites are advantaged, at least to some degree. A company which utilized slaves gained profits it would not have gained, which is then passed on to its (white) executives and its (white) shareholders. Those gains are illegitimately taken. While it is true that today there are some black shareholders and executives sharing the wealth, they are in a distinct minority (well behind the proportion you'd expect given their numbers in American society). The benefit to them is incidental and de minimis, about as relevant as saying that our obligations to slaves were fulfilled because we gave them housing and food.

Of course, most white beneficiaries of slavery have no racist motivations in their behavior—indeed, they probably aren't even aware of the racial dimensions. And no white alive today had a direct hand in creating the unjust system. That's all well and good, and it explains why reparations doesn't and shouldn't consist of reaching into white bank accounts and drawing out enough money until the "debt is paid." In this respect, reparations in the form of scholarships and education funds satisfy both interests at stake—not punishing whites for being unwitting beneficiaries of a system they had no role in creating, while still providing compensation for Blacks who to this day are harmed by racial subordination.

Bernard continues with a political critique of the NAACP's advocacy focus:

> When black kids are getting poor educations in the inner cities, the NAACP isn't going out there and pressing on that issue.
>
> When black parents are not just allowing, but encouraging their children to fail in this society the NAACP is silent on this issue.

But when a company can be shook down for cash, the NAACP has their hands out. This is simply repugnant.

No, this is simply wrong. A cursory check of the NAACP's website shows that education advocacy is one of their core issues, as well as their youth and college department. These departments are two of just five issue-specific categories in which the NAACP specifically advocates (the others being Health, Development, and Legal). To say that they are "silent" on the sub-par education received by many black Americans is false, plain and simple. Perhaps we don't hear the calls of the NAACP for improved educational access for minorities, but that I think says more about how race relations is descriptively portrayed in America today (a bunch of whiny leftist radicals complaining about ridiculous things like 100 year old wrongs and too few minorities in TV shows) rather than how most minority advocacy groups would like to hear it discussed.

But perhaps what's most distressing about Bernard's argument is that it entails a wholesale reversal of virtually every standard American legal principle. If entity A illegitimately harms entity B, and gains from it, B has a valid tort claim against A and A's ill-begotten gains. This is axiomatic in American law, and on every other issue but reparations, it is also completely uncontroversial. What is the difference here? Possibly the time elapsed (though that incorrectly assumes that the racial subordination traceable to slavery (and in general, for that matter) is something "in the past," see Delgado below), I guess. But think of the precedent we're setting: that if you can dodge liability for massive injustices for X amount of years, then you're home free. In cases of massive wrongs (and in civil claims in general), this "modified statute of limitations" argument simply doesn't fly–especially since it was our legal system which prevented Blacks from pursuing slavery reparation claims when it would have been timely. For America to a) enslave people, b) prevent newly freed slaves from recovering damages for their unjust treatment for well over a century, and then c) say they can't be compensated because too much time has elapsed is a mockery of justice.

Arguing from a different position, Senor C over at Restless Mania thinks that (in a nutshell) reparations would deprive Blacks of any future ability to claim disadvantage due to their race (a sort of "we covered that already"). Senor C implies that this would be a bad thing, so reparations should be avoided.

First off, this same argument could be used to attack any program which sought to aid blacks for past injustices. Indeed, the argument has parallels to the "backlash" attack on Affirmative Action (roughly, that affirmative action will make whites resentful of blacks and thus will ultimately be a step back in their quest for equality). Likewise, Senor C believes that actions which remedy racial subordination will remove whatever sympathy whites had for their plight—ending in "a complete reversal in the treatment of blacks at all levels of society." However, we can use the example of Affirmative Action to prove this won't happen. As University of Pittsburgh Law Professor Richard Delgado notes:

> The [backlash] argument is empirical. It holds that if you do X, something bad will happen. But stigmatization and negative stereotyping of people of color in the media and movies, and as reflected in public opinion polls, has either held constant or decreased in the roughly thirty-year period that affirmative action has been in place. Before this time, stereotyping of blacks and other minorities was rampant—groveling maids and Aunt

> Jemimas, shoot-you-in-the-back Mexicans, "ugh-want-um" Indians, and more….Stigma is in plentiful supply still, but it predates and operates independently of affirmative action. [Richard Delgado, *10 Arguments Against Affirmative Action–How Valid?*, 50 Ala. L. Rev. 135, 139 (1998)]

Second, it rather weirdly assumes that Blacks don't *want* a "complete reversal" of their treatment in society. Given the state of our racial condition in America today, I'd imagine this would be a benefit. People often underestimate the plight of minorities in America today—with anti-discrimination laws in place, everything is assumed to be made "right" (and such things as AA and reparations give blacks an out and out advantage!). They are unaware of or ignore evidence which notes that black poverty tends to last longer than whites (Delgado, at 140), that middle class blacks face more economic instability than comparable white families (*Id.*), that the children of middle-income blacks typically have worse life prospects than those of poor whites (*Id.*, at 141), and other similar issues. A wholesale shift in the racial mapping of our society could very well be exactly what we need.

Third, if blacks aren't allowed to use their disadvantaged status for anything, what good does it do them to have it? Senor C seems to think it has some value (after all, losing it would "catalyze[]… economic, social, and political marginalization"), but the only semi-tangible benefit blacks are allowed to draw from it, apparently, is white sympathy. If I were Black, I'd say "thanks for the sympathy, but what I'd really like is some concrete action to rectify the systemic racial injustices that still exist in American society today." 140 years after abolition, with racial equality still barely on the horizon, I think African-Americans can justly cash in some of their chips. And I think that even an obligation as massive as reparations for slavery only makes a dent in what America as a nation owes the victims of its racially destructive policy. Extreme wrongs require extreme remedies.

Viewpoint 2

> *"The idea of achieving justice by taking money from one group to pay another for an act that was neither committed nor suffered by the parties is a collectivist affront to the American ideal of individualism."*

Reparations Are an Insult to African Americans

Stefan Spath

In the following viewpoint, Stefan Spath seeks to discredit the need for slavery reparations in the U.S. He argues that because slavery is an institution that has existed for 4,000 years, it has spread harm universally, not just to African Americans. Refuting a consensus among economists, he also asserts that blacks no longer suffer reduced economic prosperity or opportunity as a result of slavery. Finally, he questions the practical feasibility of distributing any material compensation. To some, Spath's position doubtlessly will have much appeal. To others, his views underplay the issues of racism and reparations, relying instead on a "straw-man" type argument. Stefan Spath writes for the Foundation for Economic Education.

"What's Wrong With Reparations for Slavery," Stefan Spath, Foundation for Economic Education, June 30, 2010. https://fee.org/articles/whats-wrong-with-reparations-for-slavery.

As you read, consider the following questions:

1. What are some of the ways in which the historical background introduced by the author bears on the question of reparations in the U.S. context?
2. How does the author counter the view that slavery has impeded the economic progress of black Americans?
3. Why would the distribution of reparations be so challenging?

There has been much debate recently about reparations for slavery. According to its proponents, the federal government should award Americans of African descent financial damages solely because slavery, as an institution, existed in the United States from the founding until almost a century later.

Three principal arguments are offered: (1) The legacy of slavery has hindered the economic progress of blacks in America; (2) reparations would serve as a damage award that would rectify a historical wrong committed by the United States; and (3) reparations would give poor blacks more disposable income, which would increase their living standards and lift entire black communities.

On the surface, these arguments seem to have a modicum of legitimacy. However, because of the potential divisiveness that the issue is sure to have, it is important to closely examine the premise on which these arguments are based. To do that effectively, we must first look at the institution of slavery itself from a historical perspective.

Slavery as an institution existed on every inhabited continent of the earth for at least 4,000 years of recorded history.

Slavery was a truly global phenomenon: Europeans enslaved other Europeans; Asians enslaved other Asians; Africans enslaved other Africans; and Native Americans enslaved other Native Americans. In fact, the origin of the word slavery itself comes from Slav, as in the Slavic people of eastern Europe and the Balkans. During the middle ages and throughout the early stages of the

Ottoman Empire, Slavic villages in what is modern-day Yugoslavia (Serbia) and Croatia were regularly raided by Barbary pirates, Arab slave traders, and Ottoman conquerors in search of men, women, and children to enslave. During the eighteenth century it wasn't uncommon for up to half the slaves for sale on the island of Zanzibar, an Arab colony off the east coast of Africa, to be Caucasian. In short, people of all races, not just blacks, have been enslaved, and virtually every culture in the world has a grievance.

The only thing unique about slavery in the West is that it was abolished here. One of the earliest anti-slavery documents was Pope Pius II's 1462 condemnation of slavery as a "great crime." British abolitionists, who for the most part were evangelical Christians, championed the legislative revolution that brought about manumission in Britain and her colonies.

In the West, once the abolitionist momentum was underway, there was no turning back. This was especially the case in the United States, where the ideological underpinnings of a constitutional republic made it increasingly difficult rationally to deny slaves their rights. The abolition of slavery in the United States marked a historically significant moral high point, not only for this country, but also for the entire world. By the end of the nineteenth century, slavery as an institution was non-existent in the West and only existed in small pockets of Africa, Asia, and the Middle East.

Has Slavery Hindered the Economic Progress of Blacks?

Economist Thomas Sowell, in his seminal work *Civil Rights: Rhetoric or Reality*, concluded after exhaustive statistical research that the vast majority of whites and blacks believe there are a higher percentage of blacks in poverty than there actually are. Indeed, when surveyed, most whites and blacks believe three-quarters of black Americans live below the official poverty line, when in reality only one in four do, according to the 2001 Census.

Why is there so much confusion? Part of the problem is the perception that "black" and "poor" are synonymous. In the 1960s it was politically expedient to associate the state of being poor, uneducated, and oppressed with being black. The civil rights establishment found this association rhetorically necessary to focus public attention on the plight of southern blacks and to engage the emotions of the white majority against overt southern racism.

However, this political strategy had an unexpected impact on the emerging black middle class. According to the black-equals poor logic, when the black middle class achieved more opportunity and became more educated and affluent, it essentially became less "black." This perhaps explains the black establishment's attitude toward Supreme Court Justice Clarence Thomas and national security adviser Condoleezza Rice. Essentially, black identity was hijacked and frozen during the 1960s.

Unfortunately, the image of poverty stricken blacks in need of government handouts to get by is still perpetuated by race demagogues like Jesse Jackson and Al Sharpton, who stand to gain politically by fostering that stereotype. It is a truism of politics that charlatans in search of political power will always benefit from having a constituency with a chip on its shoulder.

Is there a legacy from slavery that has hindered the economic progress of blacks today? Let's consider the numbers. Major marketers have long constructed a black "gross national product" (GNP) from government statistics to gauge the financial power of black Americans. This is actually a misnomer since it tries to measure the total products and services consumed, not produced, by the black community. This statistic is often cited by black political leaders to persuade corporate America to produce more goods suited to the preferences of blacks. It turns out that if black Americans constituted their own country, they would have the 11th largest economy in the world.

In addition to being a wealthy demographic group (richer than 90 percent of the people in the world), blacks in America have a longer life expectancy than African and Caribbean blacks, as well as whites in many parts of Eastern Europe and Latin America. Black Americans have higher rates of literacy and achieve more postsecondary degrees as a percentage of the population than blacks in Africa. Black Americans' upward mobility from Reconstruction to the present is a testament to their creativity and ability to adapt. Reparations are not only unnecessary as a financial corrective, but they would also be an insult to the multitudes of successful black Americans who lifted themselves out of poverty before and after the civil rights movement.

Who Gets What?

If the proponents of reparations take to the courts, it will be interesting to see their principle for determining who is entitled to what. For many reasons that will be a Herculean task.

Because of centuries of migration, conquests, and intermixing, racial purity is more of a social construct than a biological fact. Intermarriage between whites and blacks in America over the past two centuries has produced a large population of individuals who defy the stark dichotomy.

Racially mixed populations in other parts of the world, such as in Latin America, have created classifications to describe themselves based on racial portions as small as an eighth. However, the practice of racial classification has evolved differently in the United States.

In an effort to deny inheritance rights to illegitimate progeny born by slave women, racist plantation owners in the antebellum South created the dreaded "one-drop rule" to discourage the courts from calling their miscegenational offspring anything but Negro. The nomenclature of this racist practice has survived to this day and is embraced by both blacks and whites, who for the most part are unaware of its discriminatory beginnings. Consider how Vanessa Williams and Colin Powell are labeled black despite their interracial heritage.

With so much racial intermixture, will those who dole out the potential reparations demand certificates of racial purity? The thought is preposterous. Another quagmire in paying reparations is that a small percentage of blacks were free before slavery ended, having bought their freedom or having had it bequeathed to them by sympathetic slave owners. Are their descendants eligible for reparations?

In antebellum New Orleans it wasn't uncommon for freemen of color to own slaves. That blacks owned slaves has been a hotly debated point. It is true that a vast majority of blacks who bought slaves did so to emancipate relatives and friends. However, there are several well-documented cases of black slave owners in Louisiana who kept their slaves in servitude for life.

Black slave ownership poses a serious conundrum in the equitable distribution of reparations. Few Americans, white or black, are familiar enough with their genealogies to know, with any certainty, significant details about what their ancestors were doing almost two centuries ago.

Then there is the case of African and Caribbean émigrés from the post-Civil War era. It is estimated that this subgroup of the black community comprises between 3 to 5 percent of the total black population in the United States. Will they pay or receive reparations?

More Reparations?

In some respects one could argue that reparations for slavery have already been paid. These implicit reparations, the argument goes, have taken the form of direct monetary transfers such as welfare payments or nonmonetary benefits such as hiring and admission quotas. Indeed, policies based on racial preferences such as affirmative action have allowed hundreds of thousands of blacks to enter universities and obtain employment based on criteria different from those applied to other groups of people.

It should not be overlooked that the greatest irony of American slavery is that the descendants of those brought across the Atlantic from Africa are demonstrably better off than the descendants of those who remained. Sub-Saharan Africa is home to some of the poorest countries with some of the most appalling living conditions in the world. Disease, war, and famine are commonplace, and corrupt governments led by military dictators and kleptocrats ensure that economic growth and development for the masses is a low priority. In his book *Out of America: A Black Man Confronts Africa*, American reporter Keith Richburg concludes that black Americans should consider themselves lucky to have escaped the squalor of what is contemporary Africa.

Not only blacks, but all Americans should feel lucky to be born in the society with the most opportunities for advancement. The American dream is not a myth but a reality—so attractive that tens of thousands of people from across the world try to make it to our shores every year. The benefits of living in the United States weaken, if not destroy, the foundation of the argument in favor of paying blacks group compensation for what happened to their ancestors.

In a system where politicians steal from Peter to pay Paul, the politicians, as George Bernard Shaw once pointed out, can always count on the support of Paul. But does this redistribution of wealth leave anyone better off? Yes. The people who receive the hard-earned money confiscated from the taxpayers will undoubtedly be materially better off. However, to judge whether such a policy is sound, one must look beyond the immediate effect and try to discern the impact on other groups.

In that respect, reparations would not be an economic stimulus because wealth would merely be shifted from its producer to someone else—no new wealth would be created. Applying the wisdom of Frédéric Bastiat in looking for what is *unseen* in public policy, we could say that the economic benefits of reparations are countered by the taxpayers' invisible opportunities compulsorily forgone. Put in this context, how could one argue that the expenditure of reparations by blacks would be an economic stimulus?

An economist as such cannot make normative judgments about a policy and remain true to his discipline. He cannot tell us how to correct the historical crime of slavery (assuming it can be corrected at this late date). What economics can teach us is that if policymakers appropriate the wealth of one group to pay reparations to a second group because a third (dead) group did nasty things to a fourth (dead) group 150 years ago, it would create a plethora of problems. Chief among them would be racial animosity and the festering of a truly debilitating mentality of "victimization" among black youths.

Are Current Taxpayers Culpable?

Of the three primary arguments for reparations, the argument for damages is the most irrational. Though slavery was widespread in the southern United States, slave ownership was not. It is estimated that less than 10 percent of whites owned slaves. The vast majority did not; they had neither financial nor agricultural resources to warrant slave labor. Slave ownership was restricted to a highly concentrated group of wealthy southern elites—the landed aristocracy.

Today we live in a country with a population of 285 million people. Because of immigration, it is safe to argue that the majority of white people in this country are descended from post-Civil War immigrants who had nothing to do with slavery.

Many ethnic groups that arrived on American shores in the early twentieth century, including the Irish, European Jews, and Chinese, were subject to severe discrimination. However, with every passing generation, ethnic groups developed the occupational skills, knowledge, and cultural norms necessary to fully assimilate and rise to higher socioeconomic levels within the mainstream American culture.

Why, then, should the descendants of these groups, let alone first-generation Americans, be financially liable to blacks as a group? In the American legal system, damages hinge on the principle of cause and effect—one pays for the damage one causes. In the case of slavery, there is no culpable person alive to pay for the crime.

Perhaps the most important error made by those who argue for reparations is not economic at all but philosophical. The idea of achieving justice by taking money from one group to pay another for an act that was neither committed nor suffered by the parties is a collectivist affront to the American ideal of individualism. People are not interchangeable pawns but individuals responsible for their own actions. Slaves and slave owners are dead, and we cannot bring them back.

Our Constitution provided the framework for legal equality for all individuals, and later legislation eliminated remaining race-based government barriers to freedom, assuring that blacks, like whites, can be beneficiaries of this great system. Thus the only solution to the race problem in America is a commitment to individualism

Viewpoint 

> *"The U.S. has yet to deal with its founding principles: genocide and slavery."*

We Need More Holistic Understanding of Reparations

Cecilia Cissell Lucas

In this viewpoint, Cecilia Cissell Lucas radically rethinks the concepts of credit and debt that inform mainstream conceptions of reparations. Arguing against individualistic and capitalist notions of compensation, the author instead posits a framework in which social groups are bound together in a web of interconnectedness. Cissell points out that disparities in wealth are linked to histories of racism and domination. What emerges is a pedagogical strategy through which these systems might be dismantled in favor of more enlightened theoretical and practical practices. Cecilia Cissell Lucas received her MA and Ph.D. from the Social and Cultural Studies program at UC Berkeley's Graduate School of Education and is currently working as a lecturer at UC Berkeley.

"Who Is Forgiving Who? Dreaming of Debt, Practicing P/Reparations," Cecilia Cissell Lucas, The Mindful Word, November 3, 2013. http://www.themindfulword.org/2013/who-is-forgiving-who.

As you read, consider the following questions:

1. The author dislikes words such as "aid" and "welfare"—why does she believe these terms are latently political?
2. How does the article characterize "holistic" reparations?
3. What are p/reparations, according to the author? How do these differ from reparations?

Some activists have been calling for debt forgiveness for the "global south" as a form of reparations. Referring to such an act as reparations helps us to understand the absurdity of the entire concept of "global south" "debt." When we examine the historical circumstances of how wealth has been accumulated by some through dispossessing others, including the processes through which so-called "lending" nations/organizations acquired the means to make loans, suddenly the tables turn regarding who needs to be asking whom for "debt forgiveness." After all, much of the capital being offered as credit (a scheme to extract even more capital!) was acquired—and continues to be acquired—through theft and exploitation of land and people. This is true both "domestically" and globally. Aimé Césaire once wrote, "There are sins for which no one has the power to make amends and which can never be fully expiated." Indeed, how can the debts of ravished natural resources and of millions upon millions of lives slaughtered, enslaved, dispossessed, raped, incarcerated and dehumanized ever be repaid? Impossible.

The impossibility is not because of the inability to change the past. The past is with us in the present. In Thich Nhat Hanh's words, "All your ancestors continue in you, and when you transform the habit energies that they have transmitted to you, you are being reborn in the past… I am present everywhere on this planet. I am also present in the past and in the future." The impossibility of repayment lies in the incalculability of life and of relationships.

Fred Moten and Stefano Harney argue that credit, not debt, is the problem.

> Credit is a means of privatization and debt a means of socialization… Credit keeps track. Debt forgets… Debt cannot be forgiven, it can only be forgotten and remembered. To forgive debt is to restore credit… it is restorative justice… To seek justice through restoration is to return debt to the balance sheet and the balance sheet never balances… You can't pay me back, give me credit, get free of me, and I can't let you go when you're gone. If you want to do something, then forget this debt, and remember it later.

It would be absurd to try to monetize the debts I feel to all the teachers who have helped me arrive at this moment where I am now writing this. And it's impossible for me to identify all the lives who have made my life possible, materially and spiritually. Except that the more I meditate on that, the more the teaching of interconnectedness takes root, with the realization: we are all interdependent, indebted to one another, responsible for one another; our debts circulate, denying the notion of one-to-one exchanges, denying the notion of interest, insisting instead on abundance and infinite incalculable indebtedness.

HOWEVER. Interconnectedness is truth but we must not blind ourselves to the particular nature of that interconnectedness, to the ways in which some of those connections are in the form of relations of domination and exploitation, to the ways in which, as the Jacksons sing, "Every breath you take is someone's death in another place; every healthy smile is hunger and strife to another child." While they emphasize that "we're all the same, yes, the blood inside of me is inside of you," they also point out that we're not yet living in ways that testify to our understanding of this truth. The material lives of some are flourishing at the expense of the material lives of others, even though we "should be lovin' each other wholeheartedly." What does it mean to love when we're entangled in relations of domination? How might we attempt to honour our debts, both those for which we are grateful (which have helped us to grow in liberatory ways) and those which horrify us (because we cannot escape our complicity in the oppression of others, which ultimately also includes the oppression of ourselves)?

In Buddhism, we learn about the falsity of the concepts we use, including concepts like race, gender, nationality, etc. However, as much as we may (rightly) resist being reduced to or defined by these false concepts, they have material and psychological consequences. In order to do away with these false concepts and their consequences, we cannot simply deny them but need to transform the conditions which give rise to them, which recreate and resurrect them on a daily basis.

The inequitable nature of our interconnectedness is highly racialized, both within the United States and globally. The U.S. has yet to deal with its founding principles: genocide and slavery. In *Decolonization: Indigeneity, Education & Society*, Tuck and Yang point out that most discussions of decolonization in the U.S. treat the concept as a metaphor, without actually addressing the central demand of repatriating the land, i.e. the non-metaphoric definition of decolonization. They caution against premature attempts at reconciliation: "the settler, disturbed by her own settler status, tries to escape or contain the unbearable searchlight of complicity, of having harmed others just by being one's self. The desire to reconcile is just as relentless as the desire to disappear the Native; it is a desire to not have to deal with this (Indian) problem anymore." And James Baldwin asserts in "The Price of the Ticket" that many white people not only resist real redress while racing towards reconciliation but expect gratitude for so-called "progress" along the way:

> Those people who have opted for being white congratulate themselves on their generous ability to return to the slave that freedom which they never had any right to endanger, much less take away. For this dubious effort, and still more dubious achievement, they congratulate themselves and expect to be congratulated—in the coin, furthermore, of black gratitude.

The racial wealth gap in the U.S. is larger than it has ever been. I don't have the space to go into all the nuances here (including issues with the categories used and the lack of data on certain groups), but would like to give one statistic from the Insight Center for Community Economic Development that analyzed the wealth gap (i.e., accumulated assets, not to be confused with income) in terms of both race and gender. They found that gender matters—if you are a woman of colour. For white women, gender plays a far less significant role. Take a look at these median wealth differences:

- Single white men: $43,800
- Single white women: $41,500
- Single black men: $7,900
- Single black women: $100
- Single hispanic men: $9,730
- Single hispanic women: $120

The past is with us in the present.

One of the aspects of the Noble Eightfold Path is "right speech." Examining the processes of accumulation by dispossession, it seems to me that the words aid, helping, giving, welfare, charity, handouts, donations, development—when used to refer to resources transferred from the materially wealthy to the materially poor—are lies. These are depoliticized words that obscure the histories and actions which created those needs the "aid" is now (supposedly) trying to address. These words silence the exploitation that enabled the capacity to "give" through stealing that capacity from others. These words imply altruism, generosity, benevolence, responsibility for one's fellow human being, and the users of these words frequently expect recognition and gratitude for such "ethical" ecogniz, adding insult to injury.

I have been drawn to the word "reparations" as a more honest alternative to these words. However, this word, too, can be reactionary, if it's used to imply the balancing of a balance sheet, thus keeping us trapped in that capitalist logic of calculable credit. In the words of three of my major influences on the topic:

> Without at least a rudimentary critique of the capitalist culture that consumes us, even reparations can have disastrous

> consequences. Imagine if reparations were treated as start-up capital for black entrepreneurs who merely want to mirror the dominant society. What would really change?
>
> – Robin D.G. Kelley

> If we think about reparations less in terms of monetary compensation for social oppression and more in terms of a movement to transform the neocolonial economic relationships between the U.S. and people of colour, indigenous peoples, and global south countries, we see how critical this movement could be to all of us… we cannot achieve political sovereignty without economic sovereignty.
>
> – Andrea Smith

> Viable reparations has to privilege systemic change and be simultaneous with helping people change ideologically. Putting restrictions on how the money can be used so that the broadest possible flourishing happens, the capacity to flourish in the largest possible sense of community. What was lost was collective. The issue isn't access to opportunity but to relationality, life, joy, sustenance, education for liberation of body, mind and spirit.
>
> – Lynice Pinkard, personal conversation

Examining the processes of accumulation by dispossession also denaturalizes the borders of nation-states, reminding us of the violence that often accompanies the drawing and sustaining of such lines. We can begin to see the lies in the word "immigration" (regardless of documentation). A reparations approach to migration might enable us to ask instead: what responsibility does the U.S. have for creating the conditions that lead people to migrate (e.g. warfare, unfair trade policies that create poverty, environmental destruction)? We might furthermore question the authority of the U.S. to determine and police the terms of migration and dwelling on the land writ large. And as Andrea Smith points out: "In questioning the legitimacy of the U.S., it necessarily follows that we question the nation-state as an appropriate form of governance. Doing so allows us to free our political imagination

Reparations as an Economic Boost

Today reparations would affect 44.5 million Americans, most of whom are in a position, or could eventually be in a position, to do far more than spend. The stimulus would lead to both entrepreneurship and investment and potential direct poverty alleviation for 3.2 percent of the total population, assuming that cash-based reparations payments would be large enough to lift even the poorest recipient above the poverty line. This would affect the roughly 27 percent of African-Americans who were below the poverty line in 2012.

Put those elements together and there is a prime case for stimulus that would both alleviate poverty directly, and provide payments to people who can either grow their investments or start or expand businesses.

Any reasonable program would start with direct cash payments of sufficient largess that it should be able to eliminate any reasonable consumer debts and allow the recipient access to retail banking services (the poor are notoriously under served by financial institutions). This assistance could immediately affect more than 30 percent of the participants in the Temporary Assistance for Needy Families program, boosting them in such a way that they no longer need to receive benefits, according to figures from the Urban Institute. The payments would be a huge boon for the states who administer the block grants behind these programs. Imagine similar reductions in the number of users of food stamps and medical programs.

"Why reparations for slavery could help boost the economy," Michael Maiello, Reuters, June 4, 2014.

to begin thinking of how we can begin to build a world we would actually want to live in."

A wholistic reparations movement is not about a one-off action of making amends for something that was done wrong in the past, or about returning to some imagined pristine state that used to exist. It's about learning from the past, loving in the present, and looking to the future while we do the work of transforming ourselves, our relationships, our institutions, and our policies in ways that might enable the greatest possible flourishing of all life. In order to emphasize the connection of past, present and future, as well as the fact that there's much work to do to even enable the possibility of reconciliation, I prefer the word p/reparations.

P/reparations is a set of open-ended processes which include apologies, material redress (for example, land, health care, education, housing, and monetary payments to individuals or groups), cultural redress (for example, through monuments, museums, curricular and pedagogical reform in education and media reform) and policies to ensure non-recurrence of harm—the latter arguably necessitating a fundamental transformation of society, including nation-state-based modes of governance and capitalism.

While p/reparations is not only about material resources, without including that component it's impossible to create the conditions for truly reciprocal and democratic relationships. Furthermore, dealing with the issue of material resources is not just a question of uni-directional redistribution of wealth, but about all of our relationships to the concept of wealth itself, as well as to notions of ownership and resource consumption. As Dean Spade argues:

> In a culture with a decreasing safety net, there is enormous fear-based pressure to save for retirement, unemployment, disability, children and other life changes. A system that individualizes risk encourages people to look out for themselves alone and steel themselves against harm, knowing that they may face vulnerability alone. What kinds of structures would our communities need to put in place together so that we could trust that we would be cared for and that hoarding does not make the world safer for us?

And, I would add, how might we go about creating such structures in ways which also explicitly address the colonial legacies of white supremacy?

For example, everyone needs a place to dwell yet homeownership (and ownership of property more generally) is one of the ways in which white supremacy has been and continues to be institutionalized. What if white people considering buying a home (or all non-indigenous people, following the point made by Tuck and Yang that settlers of all "colours" are enticed to buy into the U.S. white supremacist colonial project) were to coordinate with local indigenous groups on practices that would seek to acknowledge and begin to redress (albeit in a miniscule way) the history of land theft? Perhaps this would take the form of transferring money for a down payment to local indigenous groups, who (until the larger system of ownership is fully transformed) would assume ownership of the "property," and the would-be home-buyers would pay the mortgage and taxes in exchange for permission to live in the home.

Another possibility might be a "from-inheritance-to-reparations" campaign, inspired by the fact that the persistence of a racial wealth gap is partially rooted in inheritance practices. Expanding our notion of "kin" from immediate offspring, inherited assets might be passed on to organizations doing racial justice work. This became more personal for me recently, when my mother died and I inherited about $90,000 worth of stocks. Especially as I have no savings, having never had a job that paid more than $25,000 a year, and anticipate graduating from my PhD program with about $70,000 of student loan debt, I toyed with the idea of using this inheritance to pay that off right away to avoid paying the government more money in the form of interest. I would then pass the inherited funds on to racial justice projects as p/reparations in the form of the monthly installments that I would have been paying to the government. I decided against this approach because it would defer the p/reparations payments and because I think it's pedagogically important to undermine the sense of security that comes with wealth. Part of that security is achieved by not being in financial debt to those with the power to collect on it, part of it is achieved by knowing my parents would be more aligned with my using the inheritance to pay off my student loans. In an attempt to try to live out the idea that this money isn't mine to give, at a racially diverse gathering to discuss this issue of p/reparations, I put the money on the table for us to collectively decide how to use.

Of course, material resources are not limited to money and property. They also include time and labour, for example doing support work for racial justice organizations and movements, writing op-eds and letters to the editor to contribute to changing public discourses, having these kinds of conversations with the people in our lives (especially other white people), showing up at rallies and demonstrations, etc.

And p/reparations extends far beyond issues of material resources. Abolishing the prison industrial complex is one of the most urgent racial justice issues we face, and we desperately need to radicalize the knowledge our education system is passing on to our youth—through the curricula as well as through the pedagogies. Dylan Rodríguez analyzes the confluences of our prison and education systems, and points out that:

> To live and work, learn and teach, and survive and thrive in a time defined by the capacity and political willingness to eliminate and neutralize populations through a culturally valorized, state sanctioned nexus of institutional violence, is to better understand why abolitionist praxis in this historical moment is primarily pedagogical, within and against the "system" in which it occurs. While it is conceivable that in future moments, abolitionist praxis can focus more centrally on matters of (creating and not simply opposing) public policy, infrastructure building, and economic reorganization, the present moment clearly demands a convening of radical pedagogical energies that can build the collective human power, epistemic and knowledge apparatuses, and material sites of learning that are the precondition of authentic and liberatory social transformations.

Similarly, I would argue that p/reparations are currently primarily pedagogical—understanding that pedagogy is not just an intellectual process, but that learning is also embodied and takes place through physical, material, spiritual, emotional, as well as intellectual practice. We have not yet created the conditions for reconciliation. There are still many p/reparations that must be made before we can enter into reciprocal relationships of incalculable debt. In the meantime, no matter how many ways we may practice p/reparations, individual redemption is not possible and there are no morally pure practices—we all remain complicit with these systems of domination (albeit to varying degrees and in different ways) until they have been fundamentally transformed. My hope is that as we continue to engage, new (or renewed) visions, energies and possibilities will emerge that may be beyond what we can imagine (as possible) right now. There are no guarantees. But we owe it to ourselves and to each other to keep trying. That is the debt which motivates my dreams, which keeps me practicing p/reparations. That is the debt of love.

> Reeducation campus, rehabilitation camps, concentration camps, annihilation and extermination camps: all the death campus in which forgiveness is said to have died once and for all. However, it is in the face-to-face with the impossible—the irreparable and the non-negotiable—that the possibility of forgiveness arises, and just when one feels one has reached the end of the road in making the last step, one finds oneself walking on, making the impossible step, turning aside, turning about, turning towards. One truly forgives only when one squarely faces the unforgivable. The grand gesture of public reconciliation and redemption has its strategic purpose, but it has little to do with forgiveness. For the debt of love knows no limit; what it requires exceeds all judicial logic and processes.
>
> –Trinh Minh-ha

Viewpoint

"The cultural injustices perpetrated during the colonial era were manifold."

A Correspondence Model of Reparations Does Not Fully Redress Historical Injustice

Sara Amighetti and Alasia Nuti

In this excerpted viewpoint, Sara Amighetti and Alasia Nuti argue that Oxford University professor David Miller's account of reparations for historical injustice is lacking in the context of colonialism. His "correspondence model" is grounded in a collective national consciousness and seeks to redress historical wrongs according to their specific characteristics. For example, cases in which property was stolen could be corrected through reimbursement. The authors argue that because colonialism was a multilayered form of injustice with cultural and psychological dimensions, it is difficult to meaningfully apply the correspondence theory of redress without serious omissions. Their aim is not to debunk Miller's theory but rather to build on its strengths. Sara Amighetti is with the Department of Political Science, University College London, London, UK, and Alasia Nuti with Pembroke College, University of Cambridge, Cambridge, UK.

"David Miller's Theory of Redress and the Complexity of Colonial Injustice," Sara Amighetti and Alasia Nuti, *Ethics & Global Politics*, Vol. 8, 2015. http://www.ethicsandglobalpolitics.net/index.php/egp/article/view/26333.

As you read, consider the following questions:

1. What are some important points of David Miller's correspondence model of redress for historical injustice?
2. Why is colonialism such a complex case, according to the authors?
3. What specific problems do the authors identify with Miller's theory in relation to colonialism?

In the debate about historical injustice, there has been a shift from an individualistic conception, which evaluates whether responsibility for past wrongs and entitlements to reparations can be passed on to the descendants of, respectively, the original perpetrators and victims to a collective understanding, which focuses on collective agents, such as nations, as the proper entities that should be held responsible for injustices that occurred in the past.

One of the most influential and well-thought-out accounts of what collective responsibility for historical injustice entails has been developed by David Miller. The aim of this paper is to examine his theory of redress in light of a consideration of the complexity that some of the most serious injustices committed by nations in the course of their history display. Our claim is that taking the complex nature of such injustices into account has important implications for the way in which their reparation should be determined.[1] In order to clarify this idea, our discussion focuses on colonialism as a paradigmatic case of complex historical injustice. We explain how we understand what constitutes the complexity of colonialism and we show the difficulties that Miller's theoretical framework encounters in arriving at a form of redress for colonial injustice. In particular, we argue that in cases of complex historical injustices the principle of redress should not simply identify the proper form

1. We will use the terms "redress" and "reparations" interchangeably to refer to "the entire spectrum of attempts to rectify historical injustices." Elazar Barkan, *The Guilt of Nations: Restitution and Negotiating Historical Injustices* (Baltimore: Johns Hopkins University Press, 2000), xix.

of reparations for the historical injustice at stake, as Miller seems to suggest, but it should also include a consideration about the process through which redress is established.

The aim of the paper is not to prove Miller's theory true or false, but rather to point at some of the shortcomings that its application to real cases of historical injustice would run into. Despite its sophistication, Miller's theory does not acknowledge with sufficient depth the complexity of colonial injustice and its implications for thinking about redress. This strikes us as a significant underestimation given that his liberal nationalism would seem well-equipped to deal with colonial injustice, especially considering the emphasis it places on recognizing the importance of national self-determination, which colonialism is the denial of.

The paper unfolds as follows. We first outline Miller's account of redress for historical injustice by highlighting how it proceeds through a sort of correspondence model, according to which an appropriate form of reparation corresponds to a type of past wrong. We then present and analyse colonialism as a particularly complex case of historical injustice committed by nations over their history. In our last section we show how Miller's correspondence model of redress is not fully equipped to theorise what redress for colonialism should amount to.

Reconstruction of Miller's Account of Historical Justice

Miller's account of historical justice focuses on how nations inherit responsibility for their past actions. This means that the units of moral concern he has in mind when discussing redress for historical injustice are nations, which are understood as *historical* and *ethical* communities.

Nations, Miller thinks, exist as ethical communities consciously and actively created by a body of persons who inhabit a common territory and continuously reinterpret and reshape their common identity. However, nations are distinct from states because nationals identify with the deeds of their ancestors as their own, thus displaying a historical continuity that is unavailable to the state.[2] It is because their members share a public culture, participate in the continuous reshaping of national identity and behave in a way that can be linked—though not entirely assimilated—to their common membership that nations can be conceived as collective agents who are responsible for their actions.[3] In particular, Miller believes that this collective responsibility extends to the national past, thus encompassing an obligation to redress the wrongs that nations have committed over their respective histories.[4] Note also that he conceives of a nation's inherited responsibility for its past wrongs as having intrinsic value: it is an obligation of justice, which started in the past and is still valid in the present, independent of the current conditions of those who suffered from such wrongs.

In his analysis of national responsibility for historical injustice, Miller not only identifies the responsible agents (i.e. nations) but also explains what their responsibility entails. It is the combination of these two aspects that forms his theory of redress for historical injustice. In what follows we will not ecognizi Miller's account for its emphasis on nations as the relevant responsible agents. We will instead focus and test the second fundamental aspect of his theory, that is, the way in which he theorises what redress amounts to, in order to show that, in the cases of complex past injustices, arriving at redress is less straightforward than Miller suggests and it also needs to be supplemented by a concern about the process through which it is obtained. To do so, we first offer a reconstruction of how Miller thinks redress for historical injustices should be achieved, and, in the next sections, we test the persuasiveness of this framework through the case of colonial injustice.

In order to establish what national responsibility for past injustices demands, that is, what obligations of justice it generates, Miller adopts a simple formula; he asks what the nature of the injustice under consideration is and, on this basis, he identifies a

2 David Miller, *On Nationality* (Oxford: Oxford University Press, 1995), 23.

3. David Miller, *National Responsibility and Global Justice* (Oxford: Oxford University Press, 2007), 127.

4. Ibid., 137.

specific type of redress.[5] According to his framework, therefore, one has to analyse the form of injustice that occurred in the past in order to specify which type of redress is the most appropriate to repair that injustice and will thus recognise national historical responsibility.[6] Call this the correspondence model: redress is obtained by identifying the type of reparations that correspond to the nature of the past injustice at stake. Miller's formula also suggests how important it is for the form of redress to track the wrongness of the past injustice. It is not enough that nations take responsibility for the injustices they committed over their history by providing some form of redress; they must discharge their inherited responsibility by offering the type of redress that captures the wrongness of the injustice, and that successfully repairs it.

Now that Miller's rationale is clear, we are in a position to introduce the four different forms of past injustices he discusses and their corresponding types of redress.[7] The table below summarises them according to Miller's formula (Table 1).

As a first observation, let us draw our attention to the second form of past injustice Miller considers. Unjust enrichment (II) seems to represent an ambiguous and potentially problematic form of past wrong for the application of the correspondence

5. Ibid., 138.

6. Usually, there are two main objections against redressing historical injustices. (1) Over the centuries, entitlements to land or property might have faded away or they might have merely been superseded by the change of circumstances. George Sher, "Ancient Wrongs and Modern Rights," *Philosophy & Public Affairs* 10, no. 1 (1981): 11–14; and Jeremy Waldron, "Superseding Historic Injustice," *Ethics* 103, no. 1 (1992): 15–20. (2) The claims descendants of original victims can make are seriously challenged by the "non-identity" problem. Nahshon Perez, *Freedom from Past Injustices a Critical Evaluation of Claims for Intergenerational Reparations* (Edinburgh: Edinburgh University Press, 2012), 24–38. A detailed analysis of these well-known objections remains beyond the scope of this paper; however, we notice that: as for (1), no reference to erstwhile entitlements is necessary for understanding the injustice of colonialism, which will be the case of historical injustice we focus on (see below). With regard to (2), liberal nationalists consider nations as historical and ethical communities that outlive their members. Insofar as claimants of redress are identified with nations, it seems that the non-identity problem does not pose a fatal threat to the possibility of historical justice. Kok-Chor Tan, "National Responsibility, Reparations and Distributive Justice," *Critical Review of International Social and Political Philosophy* 11, no. 4 (2008): 451.

7. Miller, *National Responsibility and Global Justice*, 138–9, 152–9.

Table 1. Taxonomy of Miller's forms of past injustices and correlative forms of redress

NATURE OF PAST INJUSTICE	TYPE OF REDRESS
(I) Wrongfully acquired property (e.g. land and artefacts)	Restitution
(II) Unjust enrichment such as exploitation (e.g. slavery)	Undetermined restitution
(III) Wrongdoings for which there was either (i) no actual benefit on the part of the wrongdoer (e.g. internment of Japanese Americans) or (ii) no present value to the goods that were the objects of the wrongdoing (e.g. cocoa)	Monetary compensations
(IV) Wrongdoings for which the nature of the wrong remains unclear or for which it cannot be established whether the wrongdoer benefitted from her actions, and/or how and the extent to which victims were harmed (e.g. massacres)	Public apology

model because it presents us with an injustice for which it is hard to identify the correlative type of redress. The reason is that the principle of restitution that would normally apply in cases of wrongful appropriation is here discarded by the uncertainty about what (and to what extent) should be the object of the restitution. Miller suggests that the only way out of this uncertainty is to refer to a theory of exploitation that is able to define the benefits acquired by the nation through its wrongdoing and the extent to which it disadvantaged the victims. Until such theory is adopted or developed, redress for (II) remains undetermined. Rather than calling the validity of his correspondence model into question, Miller's proposed solution to deal with wrongs of type (II) proves his framework successful even in cases for which reparations cannot be straightforwardly determined (for example through the restitution of the stolen goods). Although this strikes us as a point worth highlighting, we want to consider a second observation concerning the forms of past wrongs identified by Miller. In particular, we would like to suggest that there appears to be a qualitative difference between the forms of past wrongs listed in the table above. Although Miller does not discuss this difference in any explicit way, we think it is possible to group categories (I), (III) and (IV) as capturing past injustices qua instances of a single wrongdoing (or episodic injustice). Category (II), instead, seems to point at a form of injustice, like slavery, that cannot be reduced to any specific action (e.g. wrongful appropriation) or episode (e.g. massacre), but rather refers to a system of norms and social processes constituting the injustice. In this sense, category (II) seems to encompass past injustices that displayed a structural nature in the way that Catherine Lu has defined them, that is, as historical injustices that "involved not simply wrongful acts by individual or state perpetrators. They also relied on social structural processes that enabled and even encouraged individual or state wrongdoing, and produced and reproduced unjust outcomes."[8]

Having laid out the underlying rationale of Miller's account of historical justice, we now turn to its evaluation, focusing especially on its ability to deal with real cases of historical injustice. To this end, we draw our attention to colonialism. Because colonialism is a paradigmatic case of historical injustice committed by nations, we think it offers the best ground for assessing Miller's account of inherited national responsibility.

Conceiving Colonialism as a Complex Historical Injustice

Colonialism can be broadly identified with the European-inspired project involving the subjection of one people or nation to another,[9] which took place from the sixteenth to the twentieth centuries and

8. Catherine Lu, "Colonialism as Structural Injustice: Historical Responsibility and Contemporary Redress," *Journal of Political Philosophy* 19, no. 3 (2011): 262.
9. United Nations, "United Nations Declaration of the Granting Independence to Colonial Countries and Peoples," 1960, http://daccess-dds-ny.un.org/doc/RESOLUTION/GEN/NR0/152/88/IMG/NR015288.pdf?OpenElement/ (assessed April 11, 2013).

ended with the national liberation movements of the 1960s.[10] As recently argued by Lu, colonialism should be understood mainly as a structural injustice because it was the result of a system of international structural processes and practices that legitimised and sustained colonial rule.[11] To say that colonialism cannot be reduced to the single instances of wrongs perpetrated by the colonisers is not to deny that colonial rule entailed the wrongful appropriation of land, resources, and artefacts (e.g. the Koh-i-Noor diamond seized by the Empire's East India Company as one of the spoils of war that was presented to Queen Victoria in 1850). Neither is it meant to suggest that colonial conquest and rule were not characterised by violent episodes, such as massacres (e.g. the British slaughter of a crowd of non-violent protesters and Baisakhi pilgrims gathered in the Jallianwala Bagh garden in Amritsar on 13 April 1919). However, these instances of wrongs should be recognised as part of a broader system, which allowed the subjection of the former recognize in their everyday interactions with their colonisers. In other words, it seems possible to say that, even in the absence of instances involving the misappropriation of artefacts or the perpetuation of massacres, the injustice of colonialism occurred through a system of rules and social processes involving the continuous and day-to-day foreign subjection of the colonised.

Note that once we recognise the systemic nature of the colonial injustice, we are also able to reveal its complexity.[12] This

10. We acknowledge that making the end of colonialism coincident with the rise of the anti-colonial national movements of the '60s could be problematic. Indeed, not all colonised nations were successful in their fight for independence within this timeframe (e.g. Macau gained independence from Portugal only in 1999). Nevertheless, it is from this point in time that colonialism was officially declared as an impermissible international practice.

11. Lu, "Colonialism as Structural Injustice."

12. Conceiving of colonialism as a structural injustice challenges the nation-centred framework endorsed by Miller because it points at the international and transnational processes that made possible the national colonial enterprises. Moreover, it offers a more sophisticated account of responsibility, bringing to light the different responsibilities that members of the "colonised" group (e.g. the local elite and administration empowered by the colonisers) had in sustaining colonial rule. While we think that these are fundamental aspects of past structural injustices like colonialism, we cast these problems aside in the paper and we focus on how systemic historical injustices call for a more nuanced approach to redress than the one provided by Miller. For a detailed analysis of these issues, see Ibid.

is because the colonial system was characterised by different yet interconnected structures that reinforced each other, thus enabling and sustaining the subjection of the colonised over time. In order to clarify this point, let us consider which kinds of different structures converged and in what sense the complexity of the colonial injustice was the result of this convergence.

First, as the majority of the normative and empirical literature on colonialism suggests, colonial systems featured an economic structure, which entailed the exploitation of the resources and labour of the colonised. This is a widely accepted interpretation even in spite of disagreements about the best way to understand the dynamics characterising colonial exploitation.[13]

Second, colonial systems were enabled through the establishment of unequal political relations. As Lea Ypi has recently argued, colonialism created and upheld "a political association that denie[d] its members equal and reciprocal terms of cooperation."[14] That is, colonial rule established a political structure between the colonisers and the colonised that was based on the political domination of the former over the latter.[15] It was through the building of dominative and oppressive political institutions that colonising nations could continuously exploit the resources and labour of their colonies.

Third, colonialism was maintained over time through a systematic cultural injustice. Rajeev Bhargava reminds us that a

13. To hint at the breadth of accounts of colonial exploitation, consider how some argue that it consisted especially in the employment of labour at smaller wages or the purchase of goods at lower prices than those that would have been granted in a free market. David Landes, "Some Thoughts on the Nature of Economic Imperialism," *Journal of Economic History XXI*, no. 4 (1961): 496–512. Others, instead, look at the particularly burdensome system of taxation that colonial powers imposed on their colonies. Joel Mokyr, "Disparities, Gaps and Abysses," *Economic Development and Cultural Change* 33, no. 1 (1984): 173–8. Marxist theorists have famously interpreted colonial exploitation as exemplifying the inner tendency of capitalism to expand in search of new markets. On the differences among Marxist accounts of colonial exploitation, see Robert Young, *Post-Colonialism: An Introduction* (Oxford: Blackwell Publishers, 1999), 110–11.
14. Lea Ypi, "What's Wrong with Colonialism," *Philosophy & Public Affairs* 41, no. 2 (2013): 158.
15. Ronald Horvath, "A Definition of Colonialism," *Current Anthropology 13*, no. 1 (1972): 45–57.

cultural injustice occurs when a group is denied access to its own culture. It is a kind of injustice committed in particular against collective agents because it entails destroying or coercively changing "the collectively sustained system of meanings and significance by reference to which a group understands and regulates its individual and collective life."[16]

The cultural injustices perpetrated during the colonial era were manifold. To begin with, the local cultures were either completely destroyed (especially in Africa) or coercively changed (as in the case of India); in many cases, elements of the indigenous culture that were fundamental to the national identity of the colonised were marginalised in order to promote the values and customs of the colonisers. In addition, colonising nations often created and/or reinforced social and cultural divides among the colonised, thereby exacerbating existing inequalities and promoting internal conflicts. Consider, for example, how the divide between the Hutus and Tutsis in Rwanda was widened and became a central categorisation through the intervention of German and Belgian colonial rulers. By placing Tutsis in positions of power and introducing racial hierarchies between the two ethnic groups, the colonisers restructured the system of meaning and significance in their colony to such an extent that the differentiation between the two groups gave rise to one of the cruellest genocides of the twentieth century.[17]

Fourth, the cultural injustices of colonialism led also to the establishment of significant psychological structures, which strengthened the power of the colonisers and were subsequently internalised by the colonised. By destroying or devaluing the culture of the colonised nation, colonisers constantly remarked their alleged superiority over the colonised. The historical injustice of colonialism thus entailed a full dominion over the mind of the

16. Rajeev Bhargava, "How Should We Respond to the Cultural Injustice of Colonialism?" in *Reparations: Interdisciplinary Inquiries*, ed. Jon Miller and Rahul Kumar (Oxford: Oxford University Press, 2007), 217.
17. For a history of the genocide in Rwanda that focuses on its colonial roots, see Mahmood Mamdani, *When Victims Become Killers: Colonialism, Nativism, and the Genocide in Rwanda* (Princeton, NJ: Princeton University Press, 2001).

colonised.[18] As Ashis Nandy powerfully argues about British rule in India, colonialism created "a culture in which the ruled are constantly tempted to fight their rulers within the psychological limits set by the latter."[19] Similarly, Edward Said depicts colonialism as "homogenizing and incorporating a world historical scheme that assimilated non-synchronous developments, histories, cultures, and peoples to it."[20]

Knowing the cultural and psychological dimensions of colonial injustice is essential to understand its wrongness because they helped to justify and sustain the colonial system in the first place, as many postcolonial theorists have argued. Another way to say this is that the economic exploitation and political domination of the colonised were made possible by the existence of systems of knowledge and cultural representation developed in the "motherland."

Note that by highlighting these connections, we are not claiming that some of the structural processes that enabled colonialism should play a greater role in defining it as a systematic injustice. Similarly, we are not suggesting that certain structures should take priority when it comes to establishing the appropriate form of redress for colonialism. At this stage, our observations are simply meant to point out the need to acknowledge the overlap and interrelation of different structures as a feature characterising the complexity of colonial systems and their injustice. As we explain in the next section, this understanding of colonialism becomes a crucial element of the way in which we theorise its redress not only because it reveals the difficulties involved in finding an appropriate form of redress for such a complex and systematic injustice, but also because it brings to the forefront the often neglected dimension of the process through which redress is established.

18. Frantz Fanon, *The Wretched of the Earth*, trans. Richard Philcox, Reprint edition (New York: Grove Press, 2004).
19. Ashis Nandy, *The Intimate Enemy: Loss and Recovery of Self Under Colonialism* (Delhi: Oxford University Press, 1983), 3.
20. Edward Said, "Orientalism Reconsidered," *Cultural Critique*, no. 1 (1985): 102.

Redress for Complex Historical Injustices

When colonialism is recognised as a systematic injustice characterised by a complexity of structural processes, what implications are there for the way in which we approach the issue of redress? And, more specifically, how successful is Miller's correspondence model in dealing with redress for colonial injustice understood in this way? This section develops three critical remarks regarding the adequacy of Miller's proposed theoretical framework to address instances of complex historical injustices. The aim of our discussion is not to discard Miller's theory, but rather to point at some omissions or difficulties that he should consider.

Let us begin with a question: why is it that Miller does not focus on colonialism as a paradigmatic case of past injustice, which his account of redress is meant to rectify? To be sure, the problem of colonialism emerges in his work, but only in the context of a discussion about a nation's remedial responsibility. When evaluating the kinds of considerations that may trigger a nation's remedial responsibility to correct the state of deprivation in which another nation finds itself, Miller is sceptical about the possibility of drawing a strong enough connection between colonial injustice and present poverty to ground such a responsibility.[21] In any case, Miller does not think that national responsibility for historical injustice is mainly of the remedial type; rather than being triggered by present deprivation, national responsibility for historical injustice is grounded in the need to rectify a wrong

21. Miller, *National Responsibility and Global Justice*, 251–259. In this context, Miller's critical target is Thomas Pogge who argues that one of the reasons why "Western" countries have duties of distributive justice towards the "global poor" is the impact that colonialism had on their development. Thomas Pogge, *World Poverty and Human Rights*, 2nd ed. (Cambridge: Polity Press, 2008), 209–10. Although we are sympathetic to Pogge's analysis and, in general, to those who regard the legacy of colonialism as an important problem of justice, we will not pursue this line of argument here. On this problem see, e.g. Daniel Butt, "Repairing Historical Wrongs and the End of Empire," *Social & Legal Studies*, 21, no. 2 (2012): 227–42; Jacob T. Levy and Iris M. Young, eds. *Colonialism and Its Legacies* (Lanham, MD: Lexington Books, 2011); Lu, "Colonialism as Structural Injustice," 278; and Kok-Chor Tan, "Colonialism, Reparations and Global Justice," in *Reparations: Interdisciplinary Inquiries*, ed. Jon Miller and Rahul Kumar (Oxford: Oxford University Press, 2007), 280–306.

that was brought about by a specific nation.[22] When it comes to discussing how to rectify historical injustices, however, Miller remains silent about colonialism. This omission strikes us as puzzling for at least two different reasons. First, colonialism was far from being a marginal or isolated phenomenon; as Robert Young observes, "by the time of the First World War," colonial nations "occupied, or by various means controlled, nine-tenth of the surface territory of the globe." It is therefore very strange that a theory about redress for national past injustices would not include a detailed discussion about colonialism. Second, this omission becomes particularly surprising in light of Miller's broader liberal nationalist account. From within liberal nationalism, a concern for the injustice of colonialism is quite easily expressed as a concern for the denial of national self-determination that it entailed. Insofar as Miller is able to recognise this, one would expect his theory of national responsibility for historical injustice to start from (or at least centre on) the paramount injustice of colonial rule. The fact that Miller does not proceed in this way appears as an anomaly.

One possible explanation for omitting a thorough treatment of colonial injustice could be that Miller wanted to be as parsimonious as possible in developing his account of redress. As we have shown in the first section, his correspondence model is devised around a rather simple formula that enables one to establish what is owed to the victims of past injustices in a rather straightforward way. The case of colonial injustice, however, would not seem to fit so easily into Miller's correspondence model. This is because colonialism was a systematic complex injustice, which was constituted by interconnected structural processes and not merely by the instances of wrongs committed under colonial rule. Understanding colonialism in this way requires that the principle through which redress is established be sensitive to repairing both the single instances of wrongs as well as the structures under which these wrongs were justified. In other words, one needs to think of

22. This is Miller's famous distinction between remedial and outcome responsibility. Miller, *National Responsibility and Global Justice*, 82–7.

redress as offering a reparation to the systematic structure(s) that the colonising nations created and upheld, rather than just offering compensation for the instances of wrongs they committed.[23]

On the face of it, Miller's correspondence model could accommodate this insight. As we have noticed in the first section, his theory of redress draws, albeit implicitly, a qualitative distinction between "systemic" injustices and episodic wrongs. Accordingly, one could claim that redress for colonialism under Miller's framework would not just demand the application of the principle of restitution to deal with instances of (I) and public apology to deal with instances of (IV),[24] but it would further (or especially) entail determining the appropriate form of reparation for the structures of exploitation that characterised colonialism as an unjust economic system (II). That seems correct. However, as soon as we make this move and we try to identify the appropriate form of reparation for colonialism understood as a complex systemic injustice, which was created and maintained by interrelated unjust social structures, the application of the correspondence model may present some difficulties. That is, once we recognise the systemic nature of the colonial injustice and we consider redress for its exploitative economic structure, we must also ecognizi the complexity brought in by its interrelation with other kinds of unjust structures. How can we do this through the correspondence model?

The answer would be to broaden category (II) and to include those other (political, cultural, and psychological) structures that, together with the economic exploitation of the labour and

23. This entails that even when reparations (e.g. restitution of a stolen good) are granted for a specific wrong (e.g. the seizure of the Koh-i-Noor diamond), they still need to be theorised as part of the redress for a systemic historical injustice (e.g. British imperialism in India). In other words, the fact that these misdeeds were committed within an unjust system must be acknowledged.

24. We do not mention wrongs of type (III), i.e. wrongs where no benefit was acquired by the wrongdoer, because these wrongs cannot be said not to have occurred during colonialism. Or rather, when episodic wrongs of this kind are considered as a part of colonialism, that is, in a systemic perspective, it is clear that even those instances which did not singularly bring an immediate advantage to the colonising nations were nevertheless components of a system that was not only intended but also took place to their economic and strategic advantage. Young, *Post-Colonialism*.

resources of the colonised, were crucial to the daily perpetuation of the colonial system. This, one would argue, could be easily done, as there is no principled reason for thinking that (II) should be limited to economic exploitation.[25] However, once category (II) is broadened, Miller's correspondence model would still need to establish what form of redress would be most appropriate for the colonial injustice understood in the systemic sense. Two options seem available here, but they both reveal their own difficulties. On the one hand, Miller could try to identify a form of redress for each of the structural processes that characterised the colonial system. So, in addition to developing a theory of exploitation that identifies the gains that the colonising nation achieved by exploiting the colonised nation and the extent to which the colonised nation was disadvantaged through the exploitation of its resources and labour, one would also need to elaborate a theory of, say, psychological domination that is able to determine the harm done to the colonised through processes such as that of the internalisation of racial hierarchies. Evidently, this would result in a very demanding theoretical enterprise because the colonial system was comprised of different unjust structural processes, each of which was characterised by complicated dynamics.

On the other hand, Miller could propose a "unified" theory of colonial injustice that is able to indicate the appropriate form of redress for the colonial system as a whole. Even in this case, however, the difficulty of elaborating such a theory should not be underestimated; the theoretical framework should at once recognise colonialism as a day-to-day unjust system while being sensitive to the ways in which the different (economic, political, cultural, and psychological) structures interrelated to maintain colonial rule.

One clarification worth making at this point is that we are not claiming that a theory of redress for colonialism should offer reparations for all the unjust structures of the colonial system in order to be valid. If this seems like what is required of a theory of

25. We thank an anonymous referee for pressing us on this point.

redress, it is because we are working within Miller's correspondence model, according to which redress should be determined by tracking the form of reparation that corresponds to the nature of the injustice at stake. This is the reason why the theory runs into the difficulties outlined above in determining redress for historical injustices like colonialism. In other words, the simple formula that Miller has devised to determine redress for past wrongs turns out to be not so straightforward when applied to complex injustices such as colonialism. At the same time, the problems of the correspondence model cannot simply be bracketed because, as we have already noticed, colonialism was neither an isolated phenomenon nor a type of past injustice that a liberal nationalist could light-heartedly dismiss as insignificant.[26]

A final remark regarding recognising colonialism as a complex unjust system made up by different yet interrelated structures is that such an understanding brings to the forefront an important aspect of what repairing complex historical injustices should entail. This is a concern for the process whereby redress is established, which cannot be grasped if we merely focus on its content. In particular, when we try to establish redress for historical injustices that were structural and systematic, we need to avoid reproducing the same structures we want to repair.

The significance of this point can be immediately appreciated by considering the cultural and psychological structural processes that characterised colonial rule. Precisely because colonialism was not simply an economic or political wrong but also a system whereby economic exploitation and political domination were maintained through the continuous denigration of the value of the colonised and the establishment of racial hierarchies with long-standing effects, there is always the risk for a new encounter between the former coloniser and the colonised to reactivate (at least partially)

26. The need to overcome these difficulties, while at the same time recognising the complexity of historical injustices like colonialism, is one of the reasons why, elsewhere, we have defended a "deliberative democratic" approach to redress. Sara Amighetti and Alasia Nuti, "Towards a Shared Redress: Achieving Historical Justice through Democratic Deliberation," *The Journal of Political Philosophy*, forthcoming.

these psychological structures. The seriousness of the psychological structures of colonialism, and of their legacy, prompts a concern for the way in which the form of redress should be established.

Redress for colonialism (and for historical injustices with structural components) is not merely constituted by a form of reparation that can repair the past injustice, but it also involves devising a process that forestalls the potential reactivation of the structures of colonial oppression. Therefore, the way in which redress is achieved becomes a crucial element of historical justice. In brief, a theory of redress for colonialism should be comprised of three elements:

1. The allocation of responsibility for redress on the relevant agent
2. The identification of the content of redress (or at least, of the principles whereby redress is determined); and
3. The selection of a process through which the form of redress (or its guiding principles) can be established without reproducing the structures that maintained the colonial system and still represent its traumatic legacy.

Miller's account of redress as it stands does not mention (3), although it provides (1) and offers a model for (2), which, however, has turned out to be in need of some adjustments in the case of colonialism. To redress colonial injustice, Miller's theory should not only face the complications that a correspondence model for determining reparations encounters when dealing with complex and systemic past injustices. It must also address the question over the very process of redress as a fundamental component of what repairing colonialism entails.[27]

27. Note that this holds true even though Miller's theory of redress is merely backward-looking. The fact that, for Miller, reparations for colonialism are owed independently from the existing legacy of colonial injustice does not mean that he can neglect such a legacy in thinking about the *way* in which reparations should be established. When colonialism is theorised as a systematic complex injustice, the legacy of colonial structures should significantly shape the process whereby redress is obtained, even when one believes that its legacy is not sufficient to trigger an obligation of historical justice.

"They didn't want the money. They wanted the Black Hills."

Money Won't Compensate the Theft of Sacred Land

Francine Uenuma and Mike Fritz

In this viewpoint, Francine Uenuma and Mike Fritz show how a cash payment fails to adequately compensate victims of land theft. This is illustrated in an ongoing dispute between the Sioux nation and the U.S. government. The dispute concerns the rightful claim to the Black Hills of South Dakota. Although Sioux are currently relegated to barren and poor territory, according to an earlier treaty they had been guaranteed "use and occupation" of far more valuable and sacred land. The Sioux's claim was promptly reneged upon once gold and other valuable resources were discovered in the area. Now the tribe is negotiating rent payments but face time pressures and obstacles from within. Mike Fritz and Francine Uenuma are producers and contributors for PBS.

"Why the Sioux Are Refusing $1.3 Billion," Francine Uenuma and Mike Fritz, August 24, 2011. Reprinted by permission.

As you read, consider the following questions:

1. Why have the Sioux refused money from the U.S. government?
2. What is the plan the Sioux are proposing as compensation for the theft of Black Hills land?
3. What impediments stand in the way of success of the Sioux? Alternately, what signs offer encouragement?

RAPID CITY, S.D. | Pine Ridge Reservation stretches across some of the poorest counties in the United States. Plagued by an unemployment rate above 80 percent, arid land, few prospects for industry, abysmal health statistics and life-expectancy rates rivaling those of Haiti, it's no wonder outsiders ask: Why do the nine tribes constituting the Great Sioux Nation, including those on Pine Ridge, staunchly refuse to accept $1.3 billion from the federal government?

The refusal of the money pivots on a feud that dates back to the 1868 Treaty of Fort Laramie, signed by Sioux tribes and Gen. William T. Sherman, that guaranteed the tribes "undisturbed use and occupation" of a swath of land that included the Black Hills, a resource-rich region of western South Dakota. But in 1877, one year after Gen. George Armstrong Custer's infamous defeat at the hands of Crazy Horse at Little Bighorn and without the consent of "three-fourths of all adult male Indians" stipulated by the treaty, the government seized the Black Hills, along with their gold, and began profiting from the protected land.

Driving from nearby Rapid City to the reservation on Pine Ridge, it's easy to see why the tribes want to reclaim some of that unused land — and why it was parceled as it was. Unlike the barren stretch of land that encompasses the reservation, the Black Hills are green, resource-rich, and thick with the smell of Ponderosa trees. Stretching across western South Dakota to neighboring Wyoming, they've been a draw for tourists and investors alike. In addition to gold, timber and minerals have been extracted, reaping profits for people other than the Sioux.

Fast forward to 1980. The Supreme Court agreed with the Sioux: The land, long since settled, had been taken from them wrongfully, and $102 million was set aside as compensation. The trust's value continues to grow well beyond $1 billion, but the Sioux have never collected.

One key problem: The tribes say the payment is invalid because the land was never for sale and accepting the funds would be tantamount to a sales transaction. Ross Swimmer, former special trustee for American Indians, said the trust fund remains untouched for one reason: "They didn't want the money. They wanted the Black Hills."

"The Sioux tribes have always maintained that that confiscation was illegal and the tribes must have some of their ancestral lands returned to them, and they've maintained that position since 1877," said Mario Gonzalez, general counsel for the Oglala Sioux Tribe, who has devoted much of his career to the issue.

"It's a tough, tough group up there. I'm amazed that they have been willing to sit on the money this long without taking the money," Swimmer said.

But it's not the resources alone that have fueled their determination all these years—a key reason for their lingering stand is that "the Black Hills has always been a spiritual place for tribal nations," said Lionel Bordeaux, president of Sinte Gleska University on the nearby Rosebud Reservation.

"The Sioux Indians are very attached to their lands and particularly the Black Hills because that's the spiritual center of the Sioux nation," said Gonzalez. To this day, sacred sites and religious narratives often center around the Black Hills.

"It really saddens me that we've got some tribal members that want to accept the money and they don't realize the harm they're going to do; they don't really understand why we say the Black Hills are sacred," said former Oglala Sioux Tribe President Theresa Two Bulls.

Nonetheless, leaders say the effort to reclaim portions of the Black Hills is now both principled and pragmatic: they "understand that times have changed, that they cannot remove non-members of the tribe from these lands," said Gonzalez, and are asking instead for some combination of federally owned, unused land and joint management or rental agreements. Excluded from the debate are landmarks like Mount Rushmore, Ellsworth Air Force Base and privately owned or residential land.

"We know that people are utilizing the Black Hills for their daily living, and it's never been our intention to remove anybody," Bordeaux said. "We have to coexist. But we would like to have some type of a co-management plan for certain parts of the Black Hills."

Tribal leaders are quick to point out that not only does the $1.3 billion represent a fraction compared to the monetary value of gold, minerals and timber extracted from it, it is based on value at the time of the treaty, not the present. And further, if distributed on a per capita basis across nine tribes, the money would soon be gone with little permanent benefit to the recipients.

"If you took the money, it would be [a] pittance. Our numbers are too big in terms of population, and the dollars would be expended in a hurry…in a week, two weeks' time, you're broke, and you don't have anything," said Bordeaux.

Two Bulls agreed. "If we accept the money, then we have no more of the treaty obligations that the federal government has with us for taking our land, for taking our gold, all our resources out of the Black Hills … we're poor now, we'll be poorer then when that happens," she said.

Leaders must continue to convince younger generations to adopt their long view. Tim Giago, who was born on Pine Ridge Reservation and has spent three decades as a journalist covering the issue, worries about that trend. "I think younger people aren't as attuned to it. There are many that are, but then again we're losing a lot of people."

The issue has been revived in recent years by an offer by President Obama to meet with the tribes if they could come up with a unified proposal to settle the issue in Congress. The most prominent attempt to do so in recent decades was a failed bill introduced by former New Jersey Sen. Bill Bradley, which would have returned some of the land. But in the years since, the issue has been largely dormant, and the money in Washington untouched. The administration's offer has raised a glimmer of hope that the issue could finally be resolved, 130 years later.

Toward that end, tribal council leaders have been holding a series of meetings to try to come up with an agreement to take to Washington. The Hasapa (or Black Hills) Reparations Alliance was formed to bring the Sioux tribes together to formulate a plan that could be presented to the Obama administration. A series of meetings are underway this summer and fall in an attempt to reach a unified position.

Edward Charging Elk, a member of the Rosebud Tribe, has put together one such proposal for a bill that he says is "realistic and doable" that focuses on three elements: the return of 1.3 million acres of the Black Hills, relabeling the trust money as back rent and then agreeing on the terms of future rent for the resources from the land to the tune of roughly $7 million a year. He hopes that plan will provide a vehicle for a mutually acceptable solution.

"I think the work of disunity is over now. It's a matter of rolling your sleeves up, following a very simple plan that everybody understands, and getting it into Congress," Charging Elk said.

Two Bulls sees the clock ticking as tribes scattered across the Dakotas and Nebraska try to unify. "There's jealousy, there's misunderstanding—instead of compromising, instead of discussing it and coming up with a solution, they all want their own way and we've tried to explain to them that this is very important because we're running out of time."

Giago has seen the "ebb and flow" of the conflict but says it is now at a critical juncture with President Obama nearing the end of his first term. "We have a very, very small window of opportunity to try to at least get a bill introduced, and I think we're still too far away from that. I'm hoping they can pull it together and get a bill in, but it's going to be a tight race."

And what if the latest round of negotiations doesn't yield the long-awaited redress to the Black Hills land claim that the Sioux seek? Bordeaux takes the long view of the seemingly intractable fight over the Black Hills: "If it doesn't happen, we've been here before, and we'll just back up and regroup and go forward again."

"We won the battle against Custer," he said. "But the war continues."

Periodical and Internet Sources Bibliography

The following articles have been selected to supplement the diverse views presented in this chapter.

Charlotte Allen, "Reparations for Women! Feminists Demand That Men Hand Over Cash as Compensation for Patriarchy," *Independent Women's Forum,* August 4, 2015. http://www.iwf.org/blog/2797795/Reparations-for-Women!-Feminists-Demand-That-Men-Hand-Over-Cash-as-Compensation-for-Patriarchy#sthash.mZy9mUOW.dpuf.

Ta-Nehisi Coates, "The Case for Reparations," *The Atlantic,* June 2014. https://www.theatlantic.com/magazine/archive/2014/06/the-case-for-reparations/361631.

Jean-Paul Mugiraneza, "The Rwandan case: is it possible to truly compensate victims of genocide?" *Insight on Conflict,* May 24, 2013. https://www.insightonconflict.org/blog/2013/10/reparations-for-genocide-victims.

Alyssa Rosenburg, "Culture change and Ta-Nehisi Coates's 'The Case For Reparations,'" *The Washington Post,* May 22, 2014. https://www.washingtonpost.com/news/act-four/wp/2014/05/22/culture-change-and-ta-nehisi-coatess-the-case-for-reparations/?tid=a_inl.

Alyssa Rosenburg, "Japan, World War II and the case for reparations in the United States," *The Washington Post,* July 28, 2014. https://www.washingtonpost.com/news/act-four/wp/2014/07/28/japan-world-war-ii-and-the-case-for-reparations-in-the-united-states.

Chapter 4

Should Later Generations Be Blamed for Injustices of the Distant Past?

Chapter Preface

Virtually no one is suggesting that reparations signify a current generation's moral culpability for the vicious evils committed by past generations. True, those who most blatantly exploited both the land and racial or ethnic "others" such as slave owners, colonialists, frontiersmen, and others are now gone. But their legacies remain, and this is what reparations confront. If we take an anti-racist platform seriously, we might heed the oft-cited William Faulkner quotation, repeated by then-senator Barack Obama in a speech reprinted in this chapter: "The past isn't dead. It isn't even past."

In America, this viewpoint means that the legacy of slavery lives on, both as white supremacy and white privilege. Current citizens are not being blamed for slavery when asked to be aware of and accountable for how white privilege structures their opportunities and life outcomes. Nor is blame quite relevant when blacks are summarily executed by police and incarcerated at far higher rates by the criminal justice system in the present. A radical mode of redress that undermines the lingering racism in our so-called post-racial society is clearly necessary—but how might this be accomplished?

As part of a larger and multi-layered process of social justice and anti-racism, there are two ways to move forward with reparations. The simplest is the speech act. These are official proclamations that acknowledge the past, take responsibility, and apologize. Speech acts are vulnerable to criticism for being too easy and possibly facile. Nonetheless, symbolic gestures and processes such as Truth Commissions are a critical first step. Without transparent acknowledgment of past wrongs and their implied continuity with present injustice, it is difficult to summon the political capital for material forms of redress. Although formal apologies are sometimes understood as validating victims' experience, this would be inaccurate. Wronged parties do not need nor want validation from a more powerful group. Instead, formal apologies open egalitarian space within which aggrieved groups can direct and define the terms of reparations, and push for greater self-determination.

The distribution of material reparations is less common than speech acts. Usually, those who receive reparations must demonstrate a connection to a specific sub-group who suffered directly, as in the case of Germany providing reparations to Holocaust survivors, or the U.S. compensating families of formerly interned Japanese Americans. It is a trickier case to argue for material reparations based on structural racism that is often invisible to the perpetrator. This is why cultural practices that cloak racism, such as those that would rewrite history textbooks, should be opposed.

Viewpoint 1

> *"In the white community, the path to a more perfect union means acknowledging that what ails the African-American community does not just exist in the minds of black people."*

Acknowledge the Past to Build a Better Future

Barack Obama

In the following speech delivered during his 2008 campaign for the Democratic presidential nomination, Barack Obama outlines his long-view of race in America, a position undergirded by his abiding Christian faith, and indeed, as became his campaign slogan, hope. Beginning with his personal background, Obama moves toward a discussion of Chicago pastor Jeremiah Wright. Although Obama condemns certain specific speech acts of the pastor, he is careful to not denounce the man. Obama acknowledges the disadvantage blacks face due to the reality of slavery and institutional racism. However, he also validates the frustrations of the white working class. Obama has consistently spoken out against reparations, stressing instead the importance of educational and employment opportunities. A senator at the time of this speech, Barack Obama became the forty-fourth president of the United States and the first African American to hold this office.

"Barack Obama's Race Speech at the Constitution Center," Barack Obama, National Constitution Center, March 18, 2008.

As you read, consider the following questions:

1. What was the context of this speech? Why did Obama choose this moment to deliver his comments about race?
2. What sorts of legalized discrimination does Obama identify? What does he propose can be done about this?
3. How would you characterize the rhetorical strategy Obama uses to express his core message of unity?

"We the people, in order to form a more perfect union." Two hundred and twenty one years ago, in a hall that still stands across the street, a group of men gathered and, with these simple words, launched America's improbable experiment in democracy. Farmers and scholars; statesmen and patriots who had traveled across an ocean to escape tyranny and persecution finally made real their declaration of independence at a Philadelphia convention that lasted through the spring of 1787.

The document they produced was eventually signed but ultimately unfinished. It was stained by this nation's original sin of slavery, a question that divided the colonies and brought the convention to a stalemate until the founders chose to allow the slave trade to continue for at least twenty more years, and to leave any final resolution to future generations.

Of course, the answer to the slavery question was already embedded within our Constitution—a Constitution that had at is very core the ideal of equal citizenship under the law; a Constitution that promised its people liberty, and justice, and a union that could be and should be perfected over time.

And yet words on a parchment would not be enough to deliver slaves from bondage, or provide men and women of every color and creed their full rights and obligations as citizens of the United States. What would be needed were Americans in successive generations who were willing to do their part—through protests and struggle, on the streets and in the courts, through a civil war and civil disobedience and always at great risk—to narrow that gap between the promise of our ideals and the reality of their time.

This was one of the tasks we set forth at the beginning of this campaign—to continue the long march of those who came before us, a march for a more just, more equal, more free, more caring and more prosperous America. I chose to run for the presidency at this moment in history because I believe deeply that we cannot solve the challenges of our time unless we solve them together — unless we perfect our union by understanding that we may have different stories, but we hold common hopes; that we may not look the same and we may not have come from the same place, but we all want to move in the same direction—towards a better future for of children and our grandchildren.

This belief comes from my unyielding faith in the decency and generosity of the American people. But it also comes from my own story.

I am the son of a black man from Kenya and a white woman from Kansas. I was raised with the help of a white grandfather who survived a Depression to serve in Patton's Army during World War II and a white grandmother who worked on a bomber assembly line at Fort Leavenworth while he was overseas. I've gone to some of the best schools in America and lived in one of the world's poorest nations. I am married to a black American who carries within her the blood of slaves and slave-owners—an inheritance we pass on to our two precious daughters. I have brothers, sisters, nieces, nephews, uncles and cousins, of every race and every hue, scattered across three continents, and for as long as I live, I will never forget that in no other country on Earth is my story even possible.

It's a story that hasn't made me the most conventional candidate. But it is a story that has seared into my genetic makeup the idea that this nation is more than the sum of its parts—that out of many, we are truly one.

Throughout the first year of this campaign, against all predictions to the contrary, we saw how hungry the American people were for this message of unity. Despite the temptation to view my candidacy through a purely racial lens, we won commanding victories in states with some of the whitest populations in the country. In South Carolina, where the Confederate Flag still flies, we built a powerful coalition of African Americans and white Americans.

This is not to say that race has not been an issue in the campaign. At various stages in the campaign, some commentators have deemed me either "too black" or "not black enough." We saw racial tensions bubble to the surface during the week before the South Carolina primary. The press has scoured every exit poll for the latest evidence of racial polarization, not just in terms of white and black, but black and brown as well.

And yet, it has only been in the last couple of weeks that the discussion of race in this campaign has taken a particularly divisive turn.

On one end of the spectrum, we've heard the implication that my candidacy is somehow an exercise in affirmative action; that it's based solely on the desire of wide-eyed liberals to purchase racial reconciliation on the cheap. On the other end, we've heard my former pastor, Reverend Jeremiah Wright, use incendiary language to express views that have the potential not only to widen the racial divide, but views that denigrate both the greatness and the goodness of our nation; that rightly offend white and black alike.

I have already condemned, in unequivocal terms, the statements of Reverend Wright that have caused such controversy. For some, nagging questions remain. Did I know him to be an occasionally fierce critic of American domestic and foreign policy? Of course. Did I ever hear him make remarks that could be considered controversial while I sat in church? Yes. Did I strongly disagree with many of his political views? Absolutely—just as I'm sure many of you have heard remarks from your pastors, priests, or rabbis with which you strongly disagreed.

But the remarks that have caused this recent firestorm weren't simply controversial. They weren't simply a religious leader's effort to speak out against perceived injustice. Instead, they expressed a profoundly distorted view of this country—a view that sees white racism as endemic, and that elevates what is wrong with America above all that we know is right with America; a view that sees the conflicts in the Middle East as rooted primarily in the actions of stalwart allies like Israel, instead of emanating from the perverse and hateful ideologies of radical Islam.

As such, Reverend Wright's comments were not only wrong but divisive, divisive at a time when we need unity; racially charged at a time when we need to come together to solve a set of monumental problems—two wars, a terrorist threat, a falling economy, a chronic health care crisis and potentially devastating climate change; problems that are neither black or white or Latino or Asian, but rather problems that confront us all.

Given my background, my politics, and my professed values and ideals, there will no doubt be those for whom my statements of condemnation are not enough. Why associate myself with Reverend Wright in the first place, they may ask? Why not join another church? And I confess that if all that I knew of Reverend Wright were the snippets of those sermons that have run in an endless loop on the television and You Tube, or if Trinity United Church of Christ conformed to the caricatures being peddled by some commentators, there is no doubt that I would react in much the same way

But the truth is, that isn't all that I know of the man. The man I met more than twenty years ago is a man who helped introduce me to my Christian faith, a man who spoke to me about our obligations to love one another; to care for the sick and lift up the poor. He is a man who served his country as a U.S. Marine; who has studied and lectured at some of the finest universities and seminaries in the country, and who for over thirty years led a church that serves the community by doing God's work here on Earth—by housing the homeless, ministering to the needy, providing day care services and scholarships and prison ministries, and reaching out to those suffering from HIV/AIDS.

In my first book, *Dreams From My Father*, I described the experience of my first service at Trinity:

> People began to shout, to rise from their seats and clap and cry out, a forceful wind carrying the reverend's voice up into the rafters....And in that single note—hope!—I heard something else; at the foot of that cross, inside the thousands of churches across the city, I imagined the stories of ordinary black people merging with the stories of David and Goliath, Moses and Pharaoh, the Christians in the lion's den, Ezekiel's field of dry bones. Those stories—of survival, and freedom, and hope —became our story, my story; the blood that had spilled was our blood, the tears our tears; until this black church, on this bright day, seemed once more a vessel carrying the story of a people into future generations and into a larger world. Our trials and triumphs became at once unique and universal, black and more than black; in chronicling our journey, the stories and songs gave us a means to reclaim memories that we didn't need to feel shame about...memories that all people might study and cherish—and with which we could start to rebuild.

That has been my experience at Trinity. Like other predominantly black churches across the country, Trinity embodies the black community in its entirety—the doctor and the welfare mom, the model student and the former gang-banger. Like other black churches, Trinity's services are full of raucous laughter and sometimes bawdy humor. They are full of dancing, clapping, screaming and shouting that may seem jarring to the untrained ear. The church contains in full the kindness and cruelty, the fierce intelligence and the shocking ignorance, the struggles and successes, the love and yes, the bitterness and bias that make up the black experience in America.

And this helps explain, perhaps, my relationship with Reverend Wright. As imperfect as he may be, he has been like family to me. He strengthened my faith, officiated my wedding, and baptized my children. Not once in my conversations with him have I heard him talk about any ethnic group in derogatory terms, or treat whites with whom he interacted with anything but courtesy and respect. He contains within him the contradictions —the good and the bad—of the community that he has served diligently for so many years.

I can no more disown him than I can disown the black community. I can no more disown him than I can my white grandmother—a woman who helped raise me, a woman who sacrificed again and again for me, a woman who loves me as much as she loves anything in this world, but a woman who once confessed her fear of black men who passed by her on the street, and who on more than one occasion has uttered racial or ethnic stereotypes that made me cringe.

These people are a part of me. And they are a part of America, this country that I love.

Some will see this as an attempt to justify or excuse comments that are simply inexcusable. I can assure you it is not. I suppose the politically safe thing would be to move on from this episode and just hope that it fades into the woodwork. We can dismiss Reverend Wright as a crank or a demagogue, just as some have dismissed Geraldine Ferraro, in the aftermath of her recent statements, as harboring some deep-seated racial bias.

But race is an issue that I believe this nation cannot afford to ignore right now. We would be making the same mistake that Reverend Wright made in his offending sermons about America—to simplify and stereotype and amplify the negative to the point that it distorts reality.

The fact is that the comments that have been made and the issues that have surfaced over the last few weeks reflect the complexities of race in this country that we've never really worked through—a part of our union that we have yet to perfect. And if we walk away now, if we simply retreat into our respective corners, we will never be able to come together and solve challenges like health care, or education, or the need to find good jobs for every American.

Understanding this reality requires a reminder of how we arrived at this point. As William Faulkner once wrote, "The past isn't dead and buried. In fact, it isn't even past." We do not need to recite here the history of racial injustice in this country. But we do need to remind ourselves that so many of the disparities that exist in the African-American community today can be directly traced to inequalities passed on from an earlier generation that suffered under the brutal legacy of slavery and Jim Crow.

Segregated schools were, and are, inferior schools; we still haven't fixed them, fifty years after *Brown v. Board of Education,* and the inferior education they provided, then and now, helps explain the pervasive achievement gap between today's black and white students.

Legalized discrimination—where blacks were prevented, often through violence, from owning property, or loans were not granted to African-American business owners, or black homeowners could not access FHA mortgages, or blacks were excluded from unions, or the police force, or fire departments—meant that black families could not amass any meaningful wealth to bequeath to future generations. That history helps explain the wealth and income gap between black and white, and the concentrated pockets of poverty that persists in so many of today's urban and rural communities.

A lack of economic opportunity among black men, and the shame and frustration that came from not being able to provide for one's family, contributed to the erosion of black families—a problem that welfare policies for many years may have worsened. And the lack of basic services in so many urban black neighborhoods—parks for kids to play in, police walking the beat, regular garbage pick-up and building code enforcement—all helped create a cycle of violence, blight and neglect that continue to haunt us.

This is the reality in which Reverend Wright and other African-Americans of his generation grew up. They came of age in the late fifties and early sixties, a time when segregation was still the law of the land and opportunity was systematically constricted. What's remarkable is not how many failed in the face of discrimination, but rather how many men and women overcame the odds; how many were able to make a way out of no way for those like me who would come after them.

But for all those who scratched and clawed their way to get a piece of the American Dream, there were many who didn't make it—those who were ultimately defeated, in one way or another, by discrimination. That legacy of defeat was passed on to future generations—those young men and increasingly young women who we see standing on street corners or languishing in our prisons, without hope or prospects for the future. Even for those blacks who did make it, questions of race, and racism, continue to define their worldview in fundamental ways. For the men and women of Reverend Wright's generation, the memories of humiliation and doubt and fear have not gone away; nor has the anger and the bitterness of those years. That anger may not get expressed in public, in front of white co-workers or white friends. But it does find voice in the barbershop or around the kitchen table. At times, that anger is exploited by politicians, to gin up votes along racial lines, or to make up for a politician's own failings.

And occasionally it finds voice in the church on Sunday morning, in the pulpit and in the pews. The fact that so many people are surprised to hear that anger in some of Reverend Wright's sermons simply reminds us of the old truism that the most segregated hour in American life occurs on Sunday morning. That anger is not always productive; indeed, all too often it distracts attention from solving real problems; it keeps us from squarely facing our own complicity in our condition, and prevents the African-American community from forging the alliances it needs to bring about real change. But the anger is real; it is powerful; and to simply wish it away, to condemn it without understanding its roots, only serves to widen the chasm of misunderstanding that exists between the races.

In fact, a similar anger exists within segments of the white community. Most working- and middle-class white Americans don't feel that they have been particularly privileged by their race. Their experience is the immigrant experience—as far as they're concerned, no one's handed them anything, they've built it from scratch. They've worked hard all their lives, many times only to see their jobs shipped overseas or their pension dumped after a lifetime of labor. They are anxious about their futures, and feel their dreams slipping away; in an era of stagnant wages and global competition, opportunity comes to be seen as a zero sum game, in which your dreams come at my expense. So when they are told to bus their children to a school across town; when they hear that an African American is getting an advantage in landing a good job or a spot in a good college because of an injustice that they themselves never committed; when they're told that their fears about crime in urban neighborhoods are somehow prejudiced, resentment builds over time.

Like the anger within the black community, these resentments aren't always expressed in polite company. But they have helped shape the political landscape for at least a generation. Anger over welfare and affirmative action helped forge the Reagan Coalition. Politicians routinely exploited fears of crime for their own electoral ends. Talk show hosts and conservative commentators built entire careers unmasking bogus claims of racism while dismissing legitimate discussions of racial injustice and inequality as mere political correctness or reverse racism.

Just as black anger often proved counterproductive, so have these white resentments distracted attention from the real culprits of the middle class squeeze—a corporate culture rife with inside dealing, questionable accounting practices, and short-term greed; a Washington dominated by lobbyists and special interests; economic policies that favor the few over the many. And yet, to wish away the resentments of white Americans, to label them as misguided or even racist, without recognizing they are grounded in legitimate concerns—this too widens the racial divide, and blocks the path to understanding.

This is where we are right now. It's a racial stalemate we've been stuck in for years. Contrary to the claims of some of my critics, black and white, I have never been so naïve as to believe that we can get beyond our racial divisions in a single election cycle, or with a single candidacy—particularly a candidacy as imperfect as my own.

But I have asserted a firm conviction—a conviction rooted in my faith in God and my faith in the American people—that working together we can move beyond some of our old racial wounds, and that in fact we have no choice is we are to continue on the path of a more perfect union. For the African-American community, that path means embracing the burdens of our past without becoming victims of our past. It means continuing to insist on a full measure of justice in every aspect of American life. But it also means binding our particular grievances—for better health care, and better schools, and better jobs—to the larger aspirations of all Americans—the white woman struggling to break the glass ceiling, the white man whose been laid off, the immigrant trying to feed his family. And it means taking full responsibility for own lives—by demanding more from our fathers, and spending more time with our children, and reading to them, and teaching them that while they may face challenges and discrimination in their own lives, they must never succumb to despair or cynicism; they must always believe that they can write their own destiny.

Ironically, this quintessentially American—and yes, conservative—notion of self-help found frequent expression in Reverend Wright's sermons. But what my former pastor too often failed to understand is that embarking on a program of self-help also requires a belief that society can change.

The profound mistake of Reverend Wright's sermons is not that he spoke about racism in our society. It's that he spoke as if our society was static; as if no progress has been made; as if this country—a country that has made it possible for one of his own members to run for the highest office in the land and build a coalition of white and black; Latino and Asian, rich and poor, young and old—is still irrevocably bound to a tragic past. But what we know—what we have seen—is that America can change. That is true genius of this nation. What we have already achieved gives us hope—the audacity to hope—for what we can and must achieve tomorrow.

In the white community, the path to a more perfect union means acknowledging that what ails the African-American community does not just exist in the minds of black people; that the legacy of discrimination—and current incidents of discrimination, while less overt than in the past—are real and must be addressed. Not just with words, but with deeds—by investing in our schools and our communities; by enforcing our civil rights laws and ensuring fairness in our criminal justice system; by providing this generation with ladders of opportunity that were unavailable for previous generations. It requires all Americans to realize that your dreams do not have to come at the expense of my dreams; that investing in the health, welfare, and education of black and brown and white children will ultimately help all of America prosper.

In the end, then, what is called for is nothing more, and nothing less, than what all the world's great religions demand—that we do unto others as we would have them do unto us. Let us be our brother's keeper, Scripture tells us. Let us be our sister's keeper. Let us find that common stake we all have in one another, and let our politics reflect that spirit as well.

For we have a choice in this country. We can accept a politics that breeds division, and conflict, and cynicism. We can tackle race only as spectacle—as we did in the OJ trial—or in the wake of tragedy, as we did in the aftermath of Katrina—or as fodder for the nightly news. We can play Reverend Wright's sermons on every channel, every day and talk about them from now until the election, and make the only question in this campaign whether or not the American people think that I somehow believe or sympathize with his most offensive words. We can pounce on some gaffe by a Hillary supporter as evidence that she's playing the race card, or we can speculate on whether white men will all flock to John McCain in the general election regardless of his policies.

We can do that.

But if we do, I can tell you that in the next election, we'll be talking about some other distraction. And then another one. And then another one. And nothing will change.

That is one option. Or, at this moment, in this election, we can come together and say, "Not this time." This time we want to talk about the crumbling schools that are stealing the future of black children and white children and Asian children and Hispanic children and Native American children. This time we want to reject the cynicism that tells us that these kids can't learn; that those kids who don't look like us are somebody else's problem. The children of America are not those kids, they are our kids, and we will not let them fall behind in a 21st century economy. Not this time.

This time we want to talk about how the lines in the Emergency Room are filled with whites and blacks and Hispanics who do not have health care; who don't have the power on their own to overcome the special interests in Washington, but who can take them on if we do it together.

This time we want to talk about the shuttered mills that once provided a decent life for men and women of every race, and the homes for sale that once belonged to Americans from every religion, every region, every walk of life. This time we want to talk about the fact that the real problem is not that someone who doesn't look like you might take your job; it's that the corporation you work for will ship it overseas for nothing more than a profit.

This time we want to talk about the men and women of every color and creed who serve together, and fight together, and bleed together under the same proud flag. We want to talk about how to bring them home from a war that never should've been authorized and never should've been waged, and we want to talk about how we'll show our patriotism by caring for them, and their families, and giving them the benefits they have earned.

I would not be running for President if I didn't believe with all my heart that this is what the vast majority of Americans want for this country. This union may never be perfect, but generation after generation has shown that it can always be perfected. And today, whenever I find myself feeling doubtful or cynical about this possibility, what gives me the most hope is the next generation—the young people whose attitudes and beliefs and openness to change have already made history in this election. There is one story in particularly that I'd like to leave you with today—a story I told when I had the great honor of speaking on Dr. King's birthday at his home church, Ebenezer Baptist, in Atlanta. There is a young, twenty-three year old white woman named Ashley Baia who organized for our campaign in Florence, South Carolina. She had been working to organize a mostly African American community since the beginning of this campaign, and one day she was at a roundtable discussion where everyone went around telling their story and why they were there. And Ashley said that when she was nine years old, her mother got cancer. And because she had to miss days of work, she was let go and lost her health care. They had to file for bankruptcy, and that's when Ashley decided that she had to do something to help her mom. She knew that food was one of their most expensive costs, and so Ashley convinced her mother that what she really liked and really wanted to eat more than anything else was mustard and relish sandwiches. Because that was the cheapest way to eat. She did this for a year until her mom got better, and she told everyone at the roundtable that the reason she joined our campaign was so that she could help the millions of other children in the country who want and need to help their parents too. Now Ashley might have made a different choice. Perhaps somebody told her along the way that the source of her mother's problems were blacks who were on welfare and too lazy to work, or Hispanics who were coming into the country illegally. But she didn't. She sought out allies in her fight against injustice. Anyway, Ashley finishes her story and then goes around the room and asks everyone else why they're supporting the campaign. They all have different stories and reasons. Many bring up a specific issue. And finally they come to this elderly black man who's been sitting there quietly the entire time. And Ashley asks him why he's there. And he does not bring up a specific issue. He does not say health care or the economy. He does not say education or the war. He does not say that he was there because of Barack Obama. He simply says to everyone in the room, "I am here because of Ashley." "I'm here because of Ashley." By itself, that single moment of recognition between that young white girl and that old black man is not enough. It is not enough to give health care to the sick, or jobs to the jobless, or education to our children. But it is where we start. It is where our union grows stronger. And as so many generations have come to realize over the course of the two-hundred and twenty one years since a band of patriots signed that document in Philadelphia, that is where the perfection begins.

Viewpoint

> *"If there is ever to be healing, let alone real peace and reconciliation, the truth must be spoken and justice must be built."*

Truth Commissions Force a Reckoning with the Past

Ken Butigan

In the following viewpoint, Ken Butigan describes how Truth and Reconciliation committees can be an effective means by which violated parties can seek accountability and bring political criminals to justice. Since these commissions are state sanctioned by definition, Butigan reasons that they implicitly acknowledge past wrongs—an important step toward reparation. However, as the South African example suggests, this approach is far from perfect. Although the "amnesty for truth" formula has brought many horror stories to light, material compensation is slow to be disbursed. Ken Butigan teaches peace studies at DePaul University and Loyola University in Chicago.

"Experiments with truth and reconciliation," Ken Butigan, Waging Nonviolence, March 21, 2013. http://wagingnonviolence.org/feature/experiments-with-truth-and-reconciliation/

As you read, consider the following questions:

1. How have Truth Commissions helped in bringing former political criminals to justice in Guatemala?
2. What important characteristics do all Truth and Reconciliation committees share?
3. In what ways has this approach been effective in South Africa? How has it lacked?

On Tuesday the trial of former Guatemalan dictator Efrain Rios Montt opened in Guatemala City. Facing charges of genocide and crimes against humanity, Montt is the first ex-head of state to face allegations of this kind in a national court. He ruled during a particularly bloody phase of the conflict in the early 1980s, when tens of thousands of people were killed by the state. Montt has been charged with ordering the killing of more than 1,700 indigenous people of Mayan descent. The tempestuous first day in court—with fiery statements from both the prosecutor and the defense—was broadcast live across the nation.

After the 1996 peace accords, a United Nations-backed truth commission—The Commission for Historical Clarification—found that the army and paramilitaries were responsible for 93 percent of the documented violations. Though the focus of the commission was on fact-finding and not restorative justice, Nobel peace laureate Rigoberta Menchú Tum used the commission's final report to file a case against Montt and others for their involvement in the atrocities. In January 2012 a Guatemalan court charged the former strongman with war crimes.

"Until quite recently, no one believed a trial like this could possibly take place in Guatemala, and the fact that it is happening there… should give encouragement to victims of human rights violations all over the world," United Nations High Commissioner for Human Rights Navi Pillay said in a statement. Quite likely, without the work of Guatemala's truth commission, this trial would not be taking place. Beginning with Uganda in 1974, nearly

Reparations in the Americas

The fourth summit of Heads of State and Government of the Community of Latin American and Caribbean States was held in Quito, the capital of Ecuador, on January 27, 2016 with the attendance of thirty-three delegations. The summit ended with the approval of the political declaration and the 2016 action plan.

At paragraph 64 of the political declaration the members agreed to [...] recognize, once again, that slavery and the slave trade were atrocious crimes in the history of humanity; hence, we welcome CARICOM's initiative for the creation of the Reparations Commission of the Caribbean Community and applaud the efforts of this Commission to redress the injustices of history [...], while at paragraph People of african descent of the 2016 action plan the members agreed to [...] continue efforts and strengthen cooperation among Member States to implement the Decade of the Latin American and Caribbean People of African Descent Action Plan [...].

On January 29, 2016 the United Nations' Working Group of Experts on People of African Descent ended a ten day visit in the United States to assess the situation of African Americans and people of African descent by renewing, among the recommendations to combat all forms of racism, racial discrimination, afrophobia, xenophobia and related intolerance, the encouragement to reparations to the African American descendants of slaves.

Despite this on February 10, 2016 the Delaware's Joint Resolution 10/148 while recognizing and presenting formal apologies for the State's involvement in slavery, as already done by Alabama, Connecticut, Florida, Maryland, New Jersey, North Carolina, Tennessee and Virginia, denies any willingness to possible reparations, as well as all candidates to President of the United States are doing.

"Genocide of the native peoples and slavery in olden days Caribbean," Pressenza, March 18, 2016. http://www.pressenza.com/2016/03/genocide-native-peoples-slavery-olden-days-caribbean.

30 truth commissions have been established in nations around the world. In some cases, like Guatemala, they have primarily been investigative. In others, they have sought to encourage restorative justice. While no one would claim that truth commissions have satisfactorily resolved the many fraught and painful dilemmas flowing from situations of intractable mass political violence, this relatively new experiment has begun to open up options to the traditional alternatives of amnesia on the one hand and vengeance on the other.

Four typical characteristics of truth commissions (identified in Priscilla B. Hayner's study Unspeakable Truths and summarized here) are that they focus on the past; they investigate a pattern of abuse; they are temporary, and generally issue a report when they finish their work; and they are officially sanctioned, authorized or empowered by the state. This offers greater access to information but also, more importantly, it is an acknowledgment by the state of past wrongs and a commitment to address the issues that are raised.

Today marks the 10th anniversary of the release of the final South Africa Truth and Reconciliation Commission report. While commission eventually came to be regarded as a key element of the country's transition from apartheid to democracy, Graeme Simpson of the South African Centre for the Study of Violence and Reconciliation says that it was "almost an afterthought"—a last-minute compromise between the African National Congress that wanted "justice" and the former apartheid government that wanted "amnesty." Following the 1994 elections that swept the ANC into power, the new minister of justice, Dullah Omar, tried to square this circle in a way that would try to avoid favoring the perpetrators.

As one account summarizes this novel approach, the Truth and Reconciliation Commission "dealt with gross crimes against humanity and focused on the period between the Sharpeville massacre in 1960 and 1994. Perpetrators had the opportunity to apply for amnesty for crimes committed during that period. The TRC would award amnesty if the individual could demonstrate a political objective and if they told the complete truth. The South African TRC was unique because of this amnesty in exchange for truth formula."

In keeping with the spirit of disclosure, the commission meetings—co-chaired by longtime anti-apartheid campaigner and Nobel laureate Archbishop Desmond Tutu—were open to the public and were widely covered by the media. The commission heard testimony of over 21,000 survivors of violence, with 2,000 giving testimony at public hearings.

Video reports featuring Truth and Reconciliation Commission testimony were broadcast weekly in South Africa from 1996 to 1998. Ninety-one of these broadcasts are posted here. They are harrowing television—the painful accounts of assassinations, disappearances, torture and jail, often told by surviving relatives.

The painful question that hangs in the air after most of the depositions is: Where is justice for my loved one? Even as the post-apartheid regime tried to navigate a new way forward by balancing truth-telling and accountability, that unquenchable question remained. (In the end, amnesty required meeting a series of criteria. Far more applications for amnesty, on both sides of the conflict, were turned down than were granted, as this summary from the Cornell University Law School documents.)

One of the outstanding issues that continues to confront South Africa was the Truth and Reconciliation Commission's recommendation of government reparations to victims of violence. While some reparations have been made, in general this has been lagging, which has been an increasingly pointed issue in civil society. (Even as the reparation fund grows, disbursement has slowed.)

The issue of evaluating the long-term impact and effectiveness of Truth and Reconciliation Commissions in promoting restorative justice, healing and peacebuilding is still being worked out. Nonetheless, this 40-year experiment with truth and reconciliation casts a new light of hope and possibility for breaking cycles of retaliatory violence culturally as well as individually. All of us have much to learn and build on from this growing lineage of nonviolent change.

It is a quirk of history—or is it?—that the South Africa's Truth and Reconciliation Commission report was issued the week that the United States invaded Iraq a decade ago. One accounting of mass violence was emerging at the very moment that another spasm of systemic violence and injustice was being unleashed. The simultaneity of this reinforces the need for a truthful account of U.S. policy—one that would place at its center the voice of those whose lives were destroyed and disrupted.

A Truth and Reconciliation Commission on the U.S. Iraq War could go a long way to laying bare the reality, roots and consequences of this war. If there is ever to be healing, let alone real peace and reconciliation, the truth must be spoken and justice must be built.

VIEWPOINT 3

> *"By reshaping history in this particular way, the Texas Board of Ed undermines the racial critiques of the racial generation..."*

Forgetting Is Not the Same as Forgiving

Glenn Bracey

In this viewpoint, Glenn Bracey argues that the post–civil rights movement generation, eager to appear "post-racial," seeks to rehabilitate the energetic racism of the aging "racist generation" as normative during their time. One way this is being carried out is through school curriculum. For example, in Texas, textbooks advocating Christianity, capitalism, and conservatism as superior ideologies are rewriting history to exaggerate racial threats to the "American" way of life these systems represent. In doing so, they are naturalizing the racism of a previous generation, when it deserves no such treatment. Glenn Bracey is a visiting instructor of sociology at Hollins University and a doctoral candidate at Texas A&M University, where he is completing his Ph.D. in sociology.

As you read, consider the following questions:

1. Who are the "racist generation" according to the author?
2. What motives explain why this generation may be receiving an image makeover?
3. How does the battle over textbooks and school curriculum play into this issue?

Glenn Bracey, "Rescuing the 'Racist Generation': Texas School Board Standards," Racism Review, March 19, 2010. Reprinted by permission.

For about a week now, the nation has been howling about the new standards the Texas Board of Education passed for social studies (including history, economics, civics) education. Because Texas controls so much of the textbook market, the standards Texas' Board of Ed sets have near national influence. I do not want to go into a full critique of the standards. You can find that in many places (e.g. revisionaries , and the Examiner has a brief list). All of the changes promote conservatism by suggesting the US was founded as a Christian nation, claiming the superiority of capitalism, and teaching conservative politics positively (for example, one member explicitly states that his second criterion for history books is whether they sufficiently praise Ronald Reagan).

I believe a good portion of the conservatives' curriculum battle is part of the larger white effort to rescue "the racist generation." The racist generation is that generation of whites who were adults and/or came of age during the Black Civil Rights Movement (peaking 1950-1970). I call them the racist generation, not because that generation is/was any more racist than the generations of whites before or after them. That generation, born 1925-1955, is "the racist generation," because that is how subsequent generations of whites have tacitly characterized them.

The argument goes like this: Whites who came of age after the CRM are desperate to present themselves as "non-racists." They claim colorblindness and are terrified by the notion of being labeled racist. These whites admit that pre-CRM America was racist. Slavery and Jim Crow are obviously racist, and today's whites cannot always shake their connection (ancestrally or as inheritors of the nation the "founding fathers" gave them) to pre-CRM white generations. But, young whites do not want to subject those previous generations to the ugly epithet of being racist. Therefore, they defend distant white generations (i.e. 1607 – 1925) as good people who were products of their time. "Ancient" whites weren't "bad" (i.e. energetically racist) people; they were just born at a time when racism was the social norm. Therefore, ancient whites' racism is excused. Similarly, post-CRM whites (born

1955-present) came of age too late to be responsible for fighting against the CRM. Post-CRM whites claim to be the vanguard of the post-racial era. They have no sins from which to be saved.

But "the racist generation" remains. Pictures of whites angrily initiating lynchings, police dogs, anti-busing campaigns, anti-school integration, and assassinations testify to the consciousness and viciousness of the racist generation's racism. Although post-CRM whites diminish the severity and frequency of pre-CRM racism, they cannot completely deny the history because acknowledging the racist past is essential to their claims of racial progression.

Necessary as it is to young whites' self image, maintaining the racist generation is very painful to whites for several reasons. First, to paraphrase, the racist generation represents "Jim Crow unwilling to die." Whites explain continuing findings of anti-black attitudes and discriminatory practices among whites by referencing a small collection of klan-like racists and the presence of an old racist generation. Whites claim that white racism will decline and eventually die as the elderly (i.e. the racist generation) passes away. In the meantime, old whites' pre-CRM, non-colorblind language and attitudes bring these "ugly" things close to home. The racist generation also serves as a way for anti-racist people of color to defeat the claim that racism was too long ago to be relevant. The perpetrators are still alive.

But whites now want to rescue the racist generation from the racism critique. Now age 85-55, the racist generation is aging and passing away at increased rates. The post-CRM children of the racist generation wants to send their parents and grandparents off well and remember them as kind and loving, not vitriolic racists.

Consequently, a new project is underfoot to recast the racist generation as something…anything else. We saw a first effort when Senator Trent Lott (R-MS) tried to rescue arch-white supremacist, Strom Thurmond (R-SC) at a birthday celebration. But Thurmond (b. 1902) was too old and had too public a record of racism to be successfully redeemed by Lott. Now, the Texas Board of Education is attempting to rescue the racist generation by recasting history in a way that legitimates the racist generations' racist perceptions and actions.

One of the most important changes the Texas Board of Ed made is inclusion of black militants' rhetoric in history textbooks along side that of MLK. The obvious idea being that MLK's nonviolence and soaring rhetoric cast the racist generation as unnecessarily violent and motivated only by aggressive racism. Including black militants is supposed to intimate that black civil rights activists were dangerous; the racist generations' angry response was a reasonable reaction to the extremist threat. Related, the Board's decision to defend McCarthyism by demanding that texts include findings documenting the presence of communists in the United States during the 1940s and 50s, many of whom were civil rights activists further legitimates the fears of the racist generation. The implication is that the racist generation really was under violent attack from clear enemies of America. Though unpopular, aggressive attempts to root them out, such as the methods McCarthy used, may be necessary. Finally, the Board's requirement that textbooks thoroughly teach the conservative resurgence of the 1980s-2000s—including the Moral Majority, the Heritage Foundation, Ronald Reagan, and contract with America—represents the restoration of the racist generation to the mainstream. Only now, it is sanitized of racism. Despite the fact that every part of the conservative resurgence had clear racist roots and purposes, which innumerable volumes document, the leaders of conservativism pioneered and popularized the currently dominant technique of doing racist actions via seemingly race neutral language and policies. Consequently, when whites define a racist as a person who uses explicitly racist words and has a public discrimination policy, the racist generation will no longer fit the description.

The Texas Board of Education is attempting to redeem the racist generation by redefining racism, recasting the black CRM as a dangerous movement, justifying the racist generations' viciousness and legitimating its fears, and linking that generation to more familiar entities (e.g. Ronald Reagan, the Heritage Foundation, the Christian Right) who are unquestionably not racist in very young whites' minds. In the end, the Texas Board of Ed not only redeems the racist generation, the Board resurrects it by restoring the racist generation to the larger narrative of progressive white goodness. The Board famously cut Thomas Jefferson from the approved list of 18th century visionaries because he coined the phrase "separation of church and state." The Board argues that the United States was founded as a Christian nation, whose white and Christian leadership has steadily guided the nation toward national and international success. Each generation of white whites has progressively built on the morality and superiority of previous generations.

But the racist generation was a problem for the narrative of white goodness and benevolent supremacy. The emergence of an evil, racist generation in the middle of the nation's history challenged the idea of steady progress. It also begged the questions: "Where did this racist generation come from? Did our founders lay the seeds for that generation the same as they laid for the good generations? And worst, if the narrative of benevolent, progressive white goodness/supremacy is not true, what kind of heritage is that for contemporary whites and what is their moral basis for racial domination (in outcome)? By reshaping history in this particular way, the Texas Board of Ed undermines the racial critiques of the racial generation, puts the racist generation and future white generations back into the narrative of progressive white goodness, and permanently redeems the racist generation by ensuring that future generations will have no charges to levy at them. In the memory and spirit of the late Howard Zinn, we must recognize this moment and do all we can to tell the people's true history.

> *"We accept this inheritance, this legacy of racism and inhumanity. And by accepting this legacy, we accept also the moral responsibility of putting things right."*

We Did Not Commit the Wrongs that Haunt Native Americans Today

Kevin Gover

In the following viewpoint, Kevin Gover apologizes to Native Americans on behalf of the Bureau of Indian Affairs for past wrongs and pledges to forge a new path based on mutual respect and goodwill. Gover's contrition is necessitated by a litany of misdeeds formerly sanctioned and even abetted by the Bureau. These include the forcible removal of tribes, land theft, decimation of populations and resources, and the undermining of self-respect, just to name a few. However, 175 years later, the Bureau is seeking to redefine itself as an ally to Native American self-determination and justice. Kevin Gover is current director of the National Museum of the American Indian.

Remarks of Kevin Gover at the Ceremony Acknowledging the 175th Anniversary of the BIA.

As you read, consider the following questions:

1. What was the Department of Indian Affairs, when did it originate, and what was it supposed to do?
2. Why does the author feel obliged to apologize on behalf of the Department (now called the Bureau) of Indian Affairs?
3. Does the author offer anything material beyond a formal apology? Should he have?

In March of 1824, President James Monroe established the Office of Indian Affairs in the Department of War. Its mission was to conduct the nation's business with regard to Indian affairs. We have come together today to mark the first 175 years of the institution now known as the Bureau of Indian Affairs.

It is appropriate that we do so in the first year of a new century and a new millennium, a time when our leaders are reflecting on what lies ahead and preparing for those challenges. Before looking ahead, though, this institution must first look back and reflect on what it has wrought and, by doing so, come to know that this is no occasion for celebration; rather it is time for reflection and contemplation, a time for sorrowful truths to be spoken, a time for contrition.

We must first reconcile ourselves to the fact that the works of this agency have at various times profoundly harmed the communities it was meant to serve. From the very beginning, the Office of Indian Affairs was an instrument by which the United States enforced its ambition against the Indian nations and Indian people who stood in its path. And so, the first mission of this institution was to execute the removal of the southeastern tribal nations. By threat, deceit, and force, these great tribal nations were made to march 1,000 miles to the west, leaving thousands of their old, their young and their infirm in hasty graves along the Trail of Tears.

As the nation looked to the West for more land, this agency participated in the ethnic cleansing that befell the western tribes. War necessarily begets tragedy; the war for the West was no exception. Yet in these more enlightened times, it must be acknowledged that the deliberate spread of disease, the decimation of the mighty bison herds, the use of the poison alcohol to destroy mind and body, and the cowardly killing of women and children made for tragedy on a scale so ghastly that it cannot be dismissed as merely the inevitable consequence of the clash of competing ways of life. This agency and the good people in it failed in the mission to prevent the devastation. And so great nations of patriot warriors fell. We will never push aside the memory of unnecessary and violent death at places such as Sand Creek, the banks of the Washita River, and Wounded Knee.

Nor did the consequences of war have to include the futile and destructive efforts to annihilate Indian cultures. After the devastation of tribal economies and the deliberate creation of tribal dependence on the services provided by this agency, this agency set out to destroy all things Indian.

This agency forbade the speaking of Indian languages, prohibited the conduct of traditional religious activities, outlawed traditional government, and made Indian people ashamed of who they were. Worst of all, the Bureau of Indian Affairs committed these acts against the children entrusted to its boarding schools, brutalizing them emotionally, psychologically, physically, and spiritually. Even in this era of self-determination, when the Bureau of Indian Affairs is at long last serving as an advocate for Indian people in an atmosphere of mutual respect, the legacy of these misdeeds haunts us. The trauma of shame, fear and anger has passed from one generation to the next, and manifests itself in the rampant alcoholism, drug abuse, and domestic violence that plague Indian country. Many of our people live lives of unrelenting tragedy as Indian families suffer the ruin of lives by alcoholism, suicides made of shame and despair, and violent death at the hands of one another. So many of the maladies suffered today in Indian country result from the failures of this agency. Poverty, ignorance, and disease have been the product of this agency's work.

And so today I stand before you as the leader of an institution that in the past has committed acts so terrible that they infect, diminish, and destroy the lives of Indian people decades later, generations later. These things occurred despite the efforts of many good people with good hearts who sought to prevent them. These wrongs must be acknowledged if the healing is to begin.

I do not speak today for the United States. That is the province of the nation's elected leaders, and I would not presume to speak on their behalf. I am empowered, however, to speak on behalf of this agency, the Bureau of Indian Affairs, and I am quite certain that the words that follow reflect the hearts of its 10,000 employees.

Let us begin by expressing our profound sorrow for what this agency has done in the past. Just like you, when we think of these misdeeds and their tragic consequences, our hearts break and our grief is as pure and complete as yours. We desperately wish that we could change this history, but of course we cannot. On behalf of the Bureau of Indian Affairs, I extend this formal apology to Indian people for the historical conduct of this agency.

And while the BIA employees of today did not commit these wrongs, we acknowledge that the institution we serve did. We accept this inheritance, this legacy of racism and inhumanity. And by accepting this legacy, we accept also the moral responsibility of putting things right.

We therefore begin this important work anew, and make a new commitment to the people and communities that we serve, a commitment born of the dedication we share with you to the cause of renewed hope and prosperity for Indian country. Never again will this agency stand silent when hate and violence are committed against Indians. Never again will we allow policy to proceed from the assumption that Indians possess less human genius than the other races. Never again will we be complicit in the theft of Indian property. Never again will we appoint false leaders who serve purposes other than those of the tribes. Never again will we allow unflattering and stereotypical images of Indian people to deface the halls of government or lead the American people to shallow and ignorant beliefs about Indians. Never again will we attack your religions, your languages, your rituals, or any of your tribal ways. Never again will we seize your children, nor teach them to be ashamed of who they are. Never again.

We cannot yet ask your forgiveness, not while the burdens of this agency's history weigh so heavily on tribal communities. What we do ask is that, together, we allow the healing to begin: As you return to your homes, and as you talk with your people, please tell them that time of dying is at its end. Tell your children that the time of shame and fear is over. Tell your young men and women to replace their anger with hope and love for their people. Together, we must wipe the tears of seven generations. Together, we must allow our broken hearts to mend. Together, we will face a challenging world with confidence and trust. Together, let us resolve that when our future leaders gather to discuss the history of this institution, it will be time to celebrate the rebirth of joy, freedom, and progress for the Indian Nations. The Bureau of Indian Affairs was born in 1824 in a time of war on Indian people. May it live in the year 2000 and beyond as an instrument of their prosperity.

> *"Just because you benefited from that history and I was harmed by that history, you and your brethren, may owe reparations to me and my brethren, even if you guys aren't actively oppressing us guys anymore."*

We Are All Responsible for the Past

Ken Taylor

In this article, Ken Taylor outlines a viewpoint of responsibility in which individuals are not the sole agents of their behavior. Instead, responsibility is shared among actors. For example, if an authority figure enables the transgression of her charge, both share responsibility for the wrong. Taylor extends this vision to include history as well. In the context of slavery reparations, this means that present individuals who were not around for slavery nonetheless share a degree of collective responsibility, depending on their subject position. Taylor stops short of recommending reparations but does not rule them out. Ken Taylor is co-host and co-creator of Philosophy Talk.

As you read, consider the following questions:

1. Why does the author frame responsibility as trans individual?
2. What is the author's understanding of being an "agent" of another?
3. How does history figure into this vision of moral philosophy?

"Tainted by the Sins of Our Fathers?" Ken Taylor, Philosophy Talk, 2015. Reprinted by permission.

This week, we're discussing moral taint and collective responsibility. We're asking the question, "Can we be tainted by the sins of our Fathers?" You might think that the answer is that we certainly can. Adam and Eve ate that darned apple and tainted all humankind with Original Sin. Now I know that that's the biblical theory… but, frankly, I don't get it. I have never gotten it. *They* ate the apple. Not us. Why would a loving God hold us—their descendants—responsible for what *they* did? What kind of divine justice is that??

Of course, it's not just the Bible and religion. It's also the law that can taint us with the sins of others. A parent allows their underage kid to drive the car. The kid gets in a crash and injures some people. Who do you think they're going to sue?

You could argue, I suppose, that underage children are a special case. They are not fully responsible for themselves. But they are still capable of action. And when things go wrong, somebody has to be held responsible. And since parents are responsible for the care, feeding, and nurturing of their children, it makes a certain degree of sense to hold them responsible for the actions of their children—especially when the parents are negligent in their stewardship of their children.

But it's not just with one's children that one can be held responsible for the actions of another. You're an employer. One of your managers barters promotions for sexual favors. Even if the employee is a fully functioning, autonomous adult, you, as his employer, can still be sued for his actions.

Ah, but that's because the law regards managers as *agents* of their employers. And it's quite generally true that when somebody is directly acting as *my agent*, I can be held responsible for what they do. More generally, it seems that we can assign responsibility to agent x for the actions of agent y only when there is some special relationship between x and y that enables that. We've discovered two such relations—being the parent of and being an agent of. When x is the parent of y, x can be held responsible for at least some of y's actions. When y acts as x's agent, x can be held responsible for at least some of y's action.

Perhaps we can rescue a more general principle by saying something like this. In general, I am responsible for all and only my own actions and not the actions of others. The only exceptions are when there is some special relations between me and the other —like when I am their parent or when they act as my agent.

The problem is that the so-called special cases can easily be made to pile up. And it begins to look like our general principle will get whittled down to almost nothing.

Suppose, for example, that the US decides to invade some faraway land, seizes their oilfields and installs a puppet government to do its bidding. I think I'd feel pretty outraged. But I'd also feel something else—a certain degree of shame. Now I might feel the same outrage if it were Russia doing the invading, but I wouldn't feel ashamed. Shame seems inappropriate as a response on my part to Russian adventurism in the world. Ask yourself why that is? The answer, I think, is pretty easy. I am not a Russian. And because of that I bear not even the tiniest bit of responsibility for what Russia does—good or bad. But I am an American and just in virtue of being one I can be tainted by the sins, if not of my father, than of my country.

Do I really bear any responsibility for what the US does? Isn't it the officials who decide our policies and/or the ones who faithfully and willingly execute those policies who bear real responsibility? Surely they do the bear the brunt of the responsibility. But I don't think that we citizens can fully escape responsibility either … especially not in a democracy, especially if we condone and support those policies. We can't just wash our hands of what we empower the government to do in our names. And it's not just those of us who condone and support the policies that are to some degree responsible. Even people who, say, secretly disapprove of the policies but are too afraid or lazy to openly resist bear some responsibility. Now I grant that their responsibility is perhaps more limited. They, I suspect, are only responsible for what they

What Is Guilt?

It is wrong, in my view, to make white people today suffer for the sins of their ancestors. Yet far too many of us whites—and I say this as a white Southern Christian who has been guilty of this myself—believe that chronology exonerates us cleanly. We are not guilty, but we are implicated; how can we not be? We are of this place and these people. Their story is our history. The fact that some people wish to use history as a cudgel to achieve power or to absolve themselves of their own implication in dirty doings, either in the past or the present, is regrettable, and must be resisted. However, we still must look at the past—our past—squarely, and do whatever is right to atone, even if true justice is not possible in time.

We are not all guilty. Almost no one alive today is guilty. But we are all implicated, one way or another. It's an important distinction.

"Guilt vs. Implication," Rod Dreher, *The American Conservative*, February 11, 2015.

themselves actually did or didn't do—their failure to speak up. That doesn't make them responsible for what their nation ended up doing. But it does show that they too can be morally tainted by the actions of their country in a way that an outside non-resister cannot be.

And maybe, just maybe, things can get even more complicated. It seems plausible to me that you can be somehow tainted even by actions in which you played no part whatsoever, in which you neither did nor failed to do anything relevant to the problematic actions. Suppose that for several centuries your ancestors held my ancestors in slavery. Yours got richer and richer; mine got poorer and poorer. One day the slaves are finally free. But for decades, maybe even centuries after, the descendants of the slaves are much worse off than the descendants of the slave holders. Finally, we get to you and me. Just because you benefited from that history and I was harmed by that history, you and your brethren, may owe reparations to me and my brethren, even if you guys aren't actively oppressing us guys anymore.

Or maybe you do. I don't want to say that you definitely do owe us reparations. But I don't want to say that you definitely don't, either. I just want to say that the issue is a lot more complicated than we were first making it out to be. And what better way to clear it up than listening to our episode and/or contributing to this ongoing discussion here on our blog. I'm dying to hear what you think.

Periodical and Internet Sources Bibliography

The following articles have been selected to supplement the diverse views presented in this chapter.

ADST, "South Africa's Truth and Reconciliation Commission," *The World Post,* November 7, 2015. http://www.huffingtonpost.com/adst/south-africas-truth-and-r_b_8581506.html.

Author Unknown, "Reparations: Cutting Through the Nonsense," *The Economist,* May 22, 2014. http://www.economist.com/blogs/democracyinamerica/2014/05/slavery-reparations.

Greg Barrow, "South Africans Reconciled?" BBC News, October 30, 1998. http://news.bbc.co.uk/2/hi/special_report/1998/10/98/truth_and_reconciliation/142673.stm.

Leonce Gaiter, "Are Ta-Nehisi Coates and Bernie Sanders Both Wrong on Reparations?" *Huffington Post,* January 22, 2016. http://www.huffingtonpost.com/leonce-gaiter/are-tanehisi-coates-and-b_b_9051138.html.

Jason Le Grange, "The Truth and Reconciliation Commission, Did It Fail to Resolve Conflict Between South Africans?" *Ejournalncrp,* 2014. http://www.ejournalncrp.org/the-truth-and-reconciliation-commission-did-it-fail-to-resolve-conflict-between-south-africans.

For Further Discussion

Chapter 1

1. Do you think the U.S. should address slavery with reparations? Why or why not?
2. Can former colonies in the Caribbean blame low per-capita GDP on colonialism? Has this history contributed most to underdevelopment? Or is poor economic performance due to other factors such as corruption and failed institutions? Explain your position.
3. Do the U.S. and other wealthy nations have a responsibility to immigrants? If so, should this responsibility include material assistance as well as open borders?

Chapter 2

1. Although reparations may be warranted after a war, they can also cause more instability. How do you resolve this conflict? Are there times when an aggressor has an obligation to provide reparations for former adversaries?
2. What role do you see formal apologies playing in nations that have mistreated their native populations? Are these symbolic gestures sufficient, or should more be done to right past wrongs?
3. Do you think intentions are important with reparations? In general, does a morally flawed motive cheapen the gesture and compensation? Or are such concerns irrelevant?

Chapter 3

1. Do you think corporations that directly benefited from slavery now have a responsibility to fund reparations to African Americans? Why or why not?

2. Given the difficulty of addressing the material inequities of colonialism, how might redress of more subtle cultural and psychological wrongs be accomplished?
3. Do you think native groups should accept government money as compensation for stolen lands? Or does this settle a claim too cheaply?

Chapter 4

1. Do you think the basic tenets of the American experiment such as liberty and equality for all are still operative concepts? Were they ever?
2. How effective are Truth and Reconciliation projects in coming to terms with the past? What problems do they fail to address or solve?
3. How much does history inform the present? Are we determined by our past? Or can it be overcome?

Organizations to Contact

The editors have compiled the following list of organizations concerned with the issues debated in this book. The descriptions are derived from materials provided by the organizations. All have publications or information available for interested readers. The list was compiled on the date of publication of the present volume; the information provided here may change. Be aware that many organizations take several weeks or longer to respond to inquiries, so allow as much time as possible.

Bureau of Indian Affairs
MS-4606-MIB
1849 C Street NW
Washington, DC 20240
(202) 208-3710
Website: http://www.indianaffairs.gov

The United States has a unique legal and political relationship with Indian tribes and Alaskan native entities as provided by the Constitution of the United States, treaties, court decisions, and federal statutes. Within the government-to-government relationship, Indian Affairs provides services directly or through contracts, grants, or compacts to 567 federally recognized tribes.

CARICOM Reparations Commission
Website: http://www.caricom.org

The Caribbean Community (CARICOM) is a grouping of twenty countries: fifteen member states and five associate members. It is home to approximately sixteen million citizens, 60 percent of whom are under the age of thirty, and from the main ethnic groups of Indigenous Peoples, Africans, Indians, Europeans, Chinese, and Portuguese.

Densho Encyclopedia
1416 South Jackson Street
Seattle, WA 98144
Email: info@densho.org
Website: http://encyclopedia.densho.org/National_Coalition_for_Redress/Reparations/

Densho Encyclopedia is a free online resource about the history of the Japanese American WWII exclusion and incarceration experience.

The Institute of the Black World 21st Century
31-35, 95th Street,
Elmhurst, New York, NY 11369
(410) 844-1031
Email: info@ibw21.org
Website: http://ibw21.org/contact-us

The Institute of the Black World 21st Century was conceived as a resource center and engine for capacity-building and empowerment of black organizations and communities, utilizing cooperative and collaborative methods and strategies.

The International Center for Transitional Justice
5 Hanover Square, 24th Floor
New York, NY 10004
(917) 637 3800
Email: info@ictj.org
Website: https://www.ictj.org/our-work/transitional-justice-issues/reparations

ICTJ works to help societies in transition address legacies of massive human rights violations and build civic trust in state institutions as protectors of human rights. In the aftermath of mass atrocity and repression, we assist institutions and civil society groups—the people who are driving and shaping change in their societies—in considering measures to provide truth, accountability, and redress for past abuses.

International Organization for Migration (IOM)
17, Route des Morillons
CH-1211 Geneva 19
Switzerland
Email: hq@iom.int
Website: http://www.iom.int/land-property-and-reparations-division-lpr

IOM is committed to the principle that humane and orderly migration benefits migrants and society. As the leading international organization for migration, IOM acts with its partners in the international community to assist in meeting the growing operational challenges of migration management, advance understanding of migration issues, encourage social and economic development through migration, and uphold the human dignity and well-being of migrants.

National Congress of Australia's First Peoples
PO BOX 1446
Strawberry Hills, NSW 2012
Email: info@nationalcongress.com.au
Website: http://nationalcongress.com.au/organisations

The National Congress of Australia's First Peoples is a national voice for Aboriginal and Torres Strait Islander Peoples. As a company, the Congress is owned and controlled by its membership and is independent of government. It strives to be a leaders and advocate for recognizing the status and rights of First Nations Peoples in Australia.

N'COBRA
National Coalition of Blacks for Reparations in America (N'COBRA)
PO Box 90604
Washington, DC 20090
(202) 291-8400
Email: NationalNCOBRA@aol.com
Website: http://ncobra.org/aboutus/index.html

The National Coalition of Blacks for Reparations in America is a mass-based coalition organized for the sole purpose of obtaining reparations for African descendants in the United States.

Poverty and Race Research and Action Council (PRRAC)
1200 18th Street NW, #200
Washington, DC 20036
(202) 906-8023
Email: info@prrac.org
Website: http://www.prrac.org/full_text.php?%20text_id=649&item_id=6623&newsletter_id=17

The Poverty and Race Research Action Council (PRRAC) is a civil rights policy organization convened by major civil rights, civil liberties, and anti-poverty groups in 1989-90. PRRAC's primary mission is to help connect advocates with social scientists working on race and poverty issues, and to promote a research-based advocacy strategy on structural inequality issues. PRRAC sponsors social science research, provides technical assistance, and convenes advocates and researchers around particular race and poverty issues.

Truth and Reconciliation Commission
Email: tmokushane@justice.gov.za
Website: http://www.justice.gov.za/trc/

The South African Truth and Reconciliation Commission (TRC) was set up by the Government of National Unity to help deal with what happened under apartheid. The conflict during this period resulted in violence and human rights abuses from all sides. No section of society escaped these abuses.

Bibliography of Books

Michelle Alexander. *The New Jim Crow: Mass Incarceration in the Age of Colorblindness*. New York, NY: New Press, 2016.

Hillary Beckles. *Britain's Black Debt: Reparations for Carribbean Slavery and Native Genocide*. Kingston, Jamaica: University of West Indies Press, 2013.

Boris Bittker. *The Case for Black Reparations*. New York, NY: Penguin, 2003.

Alfred Brophry. *Reconstructing the Dreamland: The Tulsa Riot of 1921: Race, Reparations, and Reconciliation*. Oxford, England: Oxford University Press 2002.

Gene Brown. *Reparations for Slavery and Disenfranchisement to African Americans*. Bloomington, IN: Xlibris Corporation, 2009.

Claudia Card and Armen Marsobian. *Genocide's Aftermath: Responsbility and Repair*. Malden, MA: Blackwell, 2007.

Ta-Nehsi Coates. *Between the World and M*e. New York, NY: Random House, 2015.

Angelo J. Cortlett. *Race, Racism, and Reparations*. Ithaca, NY: Cornell University Press, 2003.

Joe R. Feagin. *Racist America: Roots, Current Realities, and Future Reparations*. New York, NY: Routledge, 2014.

Carla Ferstman, Mariana Goetz, and Alan Stephens. *Reparations for Victims of Genocide, War Crimes, and Crimes Against Humanity: Systems in Place and Systems in the Making*. Leiden, Netherlands: Brill, 2009.

Rhoda Howard-Hassman. *Reparations to Africa*. Pittsburgh, PA: University of Pennsylvania Press, 2011.

Regula Ludi. *Reparations for Nazi Victims in Postwar Europe*. Cambridge, England: Cambridge University Press, 2012.

Connor McCarthy. *Reparations and Victim Support in the International Criminal Court*. New York, NY: Cambridge University Press, 2012.

Alondra Nelson. *The Social Life of DNA: Race, Reparations, and Reconciliation after the Genome*. Boston, MA: Beacon Press, 2016.

Nahshon Perez. *Freedom from Past Injustices: A Critical Evaluation of Claims for Intergenerational Reparations*. Edinburgh, Scotland: Edinburgh University Press, 2012.

Peipei Qiu, Zhiliang Su, and Lifei Chen. *Chinese Comfort Women: Testimonies from Imperial Japan's Sex Slaves*. Hong Kong, China: Hong Kong University Press, 2014.

Ronald Salzbeger. *Reparations for Slavery: A Reader*. New York, NY: Rowman & Littlefield Inc., 2004.

Mira Shimabukuro. *Relocating Authority: Japanese Americans Writing to Redress Mass Incarceration*. Boulder, CO: Colorado University Press, 2015.

Susan Slyomovics. *How to Accept German Reparations*. Philadelphia, PA: University of Pennsylvania Press, 2014.

Richard Vernon. *Historical Redress: Must We Pay for the Past?* New York, NY: Continuum, 2012.

Joanna Vollhardt. *Aftermath of Genocide: Psychological Perspectives*. Hoboken, NJ: John Wiley & Sons, Inc., 2013.

Richard A.Wilson. *The Politics of Truth and Reconciliation in South Africa: Legitimizing the Post-Apartheid State*. Cambridge, England: Cambridge University Press, 2006.

Stephanie Wolf. *The Politics of Reparations and Apologies*. New York, NY: Springer New York, 2014.

Eric Yamamoto. *Race, Rights and Reparations: Law and the Japanese American Internment*. Frederick, MD: Wolters Kluwer Law &Business, 2013.

Index